DEBRETT'S
GUIDE TO
BUSINESS ETIQUETTE

D1555765

DEBRETT'S GUIDE TO BUSINESS ETIQUETTE

The Complete Book of Modern Business Practice and Etiquette

Nicholas Yapp

HEADLINE

First published in 1994
by HEADLINE BOOK PUBLISHING

Reprinted in this edition in 1994
HEADLINE BOOK PUBLISHING

10 9 8 7 6 5 4 3 2 1

British Library Cataloguing in Publication Data

Yapp, Nick
Debrett's Guide to Business Etiquette
New ed
I. Title
395.52

ISBN 0–7472–0975–8

Typeset by
Letterpart Limited, Reigate, Surrey

Printed and bound in Great Britain by
Mackays of Chatham PLC, Chatham, Kent

HEADLINE BOOK PUBLISHING
A division of Hodder Headline PLC
338 Euston Road
London NW1 3BH

To Roger Houghton
in admiration of both his business and his etiquette

Contents

Introduction

If we don't like the way we are treated in our local pub, cinema or service station, we take our custom elsewhere. If we don't like the hotel we're staying at, we move. If we don't like our nearest supermarket, we shop at another. If we don't like the atmosphere in our office, our place of work, we are denied this freedom of choice. We can't go elsewhere – not in an age of mass unemployment. We have to stick with our job and stick with our office colleagues.

Our business clients don't. If the office has an aura of rudeness, moodiness, or sullen discontent, *they* will go elsewhere. Few of us still have a monopoly of the goods or services we wish to sell. The industrial and commercial development of so much of the world has meant that our customers can always find an alternative if they don't want to deal with us.

It helps to be courteous. It helps to have good business manners. And more and more it helps to be aware of the business customs and concerns of other people. If we're called for a job interview, we usually do a little homework. We find out as much as we can about the firm, the job, the expectations. Is it the sort of place where everyone wears suits and squalor is frowned upon? Is it perhaps in a sartorial and conventional timewarp? There are still some companies, departments and offices that prefer women to wear skirts rather than trousers. There are still some employers who insist upon it. Now, we are not concerned here with whether or not this is a stupid or outmoded or sexist practice. That's a battle that may have to be fought, but we can't fight it there and

1

then, in the office, or at the interview, and pretend that this is good business etiquette. Etiquette isn't necessarily right or wrong. It is simply the established, the accepted practice. If we go against that practice, even if we are morally right, we are going to be considered rude, or, at best, a little strange. There is a story, too good to be checked, that an ardent pacifist once applied for the post of Curator of the Imperial War Museum. At the interview, after the panel had recovered from the shock of seeing a candidate garbed in sloppy sweater, jeans and sandals, he was asked what he would do if appointed to the post.

'I'd close the place,' he said.

It was an honest and truthful answer, but it didn't fall within the framework of established practice. He didn't get the job.

The aim of this book is to provide a guide to correct behaviour. Much of it, hopefully, comes under the heading of 'Common Sense', but at times of stress (important meetings, negotiations or interviews), our common sense may be pushed aside by other, atavistic instincts and emotions. It helps, therefore, to prepare for such trials beforehand, by considering how we should behave in such situations, rather than simply leaving it to fate and the heart.

Each chapter deals with a separate aspect of business life – telephone techniques, office practice and malpractice, meetings, office socials, etc. In many cases ten point lists have been drawn up to cover the important aspects of particular topics. If any reader wonders why ten (rather than nine or eleven), it's because it seems to me that ten is the maximum number of items of information that anyone can digest at one reading. Ten Commandments have been enough to dictate morality for the entire Judaeo-Christian world for a couple of thousand years, so ten suggestions should cover how to write a reasonable business letter.

Part Two of the book (Chapters 19 to 23) covers foreign ground. Increasingly, Britain has had to act as a nation of international shopkeepers, buying and selling all round the world. When only a few nations could design and build a fighter aircraft or a power station or a hospital complex, it was possible to adopt a very cavalier attitude to the rest of the world and not care about Japanese or Korean customs and culture, or how to dress in Arab society, or about German or Spanish sensitivities.

Today, all is very different. There is a great deal of competition, and the tender isn't always granted to the cheapest bidder. It often goes to bidders whose negotiations have been the most trouble free, who have shown the most sympathetic understanding of the traditions and manners of the country in which they are dealing, who (to put it at its lowest) have trodden on the fewest toes. Most languages have their own equivalent of the French *faux pas*. Every culture has its correct way of behaving. Every office has its code, written or unwritten, which outlines what can and can't be done. Whatever the language, whatever the setting, whatever the problem – I hope this book helps.

PART ONE

CHAPTER 1

What is an office?

To George F Babbitt, as to most prosperous citizens of
Zenith, his motor car was poetry and tragedy, love and
heroism. The office was his pirate ship . . .

SINCLAIR LEWIS – *Babbitt*

This book is mainly concerned with the sort of business that
takes place within an office, although it is appreciated that a
great deal of business takes place on aeroplanes, in restaurants, in executive boxes at Lords and Ascot, and possibly
during intervals at Glyndebourne. All such deals, however,
are almost certain to come to an office at some time or other
– they are office related. This book is not, sadly, about the
etiquette of the second hand car lot, the saloon bar of 'The
Black Horse and Harrow' at Catford, or the back of the
popular stand at Bogside.

Business Etiquette, therefore, becomes almost synonymous with Office Etiquette – hence the question posed at
the beginning of this chapter. To understand how to organise an office and how to behave in an office we have first to
establish certain facts about what an office is. And these
facts are:

1. That it's a place where a number of people come
   together to work for a common purpose.
2. That it has a hierarchy, however gently that structure
   sits upon the office.
3. That most people attend that office mainly (if not
   entirely) because they are paid to do so.
4. That very few of them had any say in who else is
   employed in that office.

An office isn't a social gathering of friends. It isn't a club or a hotel or a house of charity. It is a place that has to have rules and procedures and practices that are clearly known to all who work there; and the bigger it is, the more people it employs, the more difficult it is to establish unanimity of thought about such rules and procedures. This is why the smooth running of any such office is enormously helped by the occupants understanding and practising good business etiquette. Few offices have guides to good business etiquette printed on company notepaper and pinned to their office walls (maybe it wouldn't be a bad idea if they did so), but most hope that some kind of common-sense approach to politeness and tolerance will prevail. There is, however, a great deal more to the smooth running of offices than common sense.

Offices are places of pressure, of stress and strain, of great hopes and bitter disappointments. They are also places where people fall in love, or think they fall in love, where they become jealous, sullen, paranoid, slovenly, irascible, irrational and apparently irremovable. They are places where people reveal their inner turmoils, by cluttering their desks in such a way that they resemble a Council tip and by failing to meet deadlines and proving themselves dreadfully unreliable. They are places where life itself takes on a glorious hue when contracts are gained and orders flood in. They are places that take on a morgue-like chill when redundancy notices are flying. They are always busy places – with work, hopefully, but certainly with gossip and giggling, rancour and recrimination. We take our hopes and our fears to the office, and we pick up some more of both once we get there.

Above all, an office is a place where we are judged – by our juniors, our peers and our bosses. If we do well, if we fit in, if we become prized members of staff, then all is very pleasant, and we may look forward to promotion. If we are a pain in the neck, then we may be the first to go when cuts have to be made. We may be great at our job, but we have also to be decent, civilised, polite human beings, producing office-appropriate behaviour at our place of work.

'O wad some Pow'r the giftie gie us,' sang dear old Robert Burns, 'To see coursels as others see us.' He was singing 'To a Louse' at the time, but the wish is relevant to office life. We should regularly try to imagine how we appear to others at the office – not just our boss, but to the commissionaire, the receptionist, the messenger, whoever makes the tea and coffee, and to the caretaker. If we're going to be poetical in this paragraph, we may remember the words of John Donne: 'No man (or woman) is an Island, entire of itself; every man is a piece of the Continent, a part of the main.' No matter how important we are, we have to get on with our colleagues or the office will not run efficiently and comfortably. No matter how unimportant we are, we must be treated with respect, or the atmosphere in the office will turn sour, sooner or later.

Pre-eminently, an office is a place where there are seniors and juniors, employers and employees, those who make the rules and those who have to follow them. It's all set up to become a classic 'us' and 'them' location. It doesn't take much (or many) for things to go very wrong. A thoughtless or high-handed remark can result in a previously conscientious worker deciding that he or she is never again going to put the company first. A misplaced reluctance to tell the office Romeo and Juliet to cool their passion can result in a whole mess of bickering and resentment on the part of others, and a lot of damaging gossip. A failure to greet a visitor promptly with due politeness will tarnish the company's image – perhaps with disastrous results. And, once things start going wrong, they have a habit of getting worse. Every institution can become a breeding place for bad feelings, can develop a bad atmosphere, can slip into bad habits – hospitals, schools, barracks, barristers' chambers, hotels, department stores. Even convents are not immune. Many institutions try to limit damage by having elaborate systems of rules covering behaviour. Few offices go this far, but most rely on an unwritten code of conduct – an understanding as to how we should behave towards each other. This is the foundation of business etiquette.

What is Business Etiquette?

Business etiquette covers most of the everyday practicalities of office life. It's simply a code of manners which, it is suggested, helps to regulate how people behave in an office setting. It's not just about standing up when certain people enter the room, or who should sit first when a group goes into a meeting. It's about how to behave towards clients on the phone – including rude ones – how to communicate and what to communicate, how to make an excuse for lateness and how to deal with that excuse, how to introduce clients to colleagues, how to give and take criticism, when and how to organise a business lunch, how to treat male and female colleagues, how to deal with office pests, and what to wear. It's about making sure that, whatever the occasion, we perform in such a way that our endeavours are crowned with success, however modest or ambitious they are. And we are most likely to perform to the best of our ability if we have some good idea of what is expected of us, and by whom, and why.

The business world has become horrendously competitive in the last ten years. Old loyalties have been trampled underfoot. Those of us who felt we were owed a favour or two have been shocked to find that favour unforthcoming. All is fair in business. Customers shop around. We cannot risk turning away a potential client by sloppy telephone manners or presentation. We have to try to get the best out of everyone on the staff. We have to promote good practice. We have to know how to greet visitors from Japan, Korea, China, the Middle East, Eastern Europe and the United States. We have to know something of the cultures of those countries, of their religions, of their morality, of how they treat women, of their business practices. We are not going to pretend that we are Japanese or Korean, but that we are sensitive to their way of thinking and acting, and, especially, to their way of doing business. Our performance has to have that edge to it, that polish, that suggestion that we know how to conduct ourselves in business negotiations.

CHAPTER 2

Getting into business

By our first strange and fatal interview,
By all desires which thereof did ensue,
By our long starving hopes, by that remorse
Which my words' masculine persuasive force,
Begot in thee . . .

JOHN DONNE
– Elegy XVI: On his Mistress

Most people make their entry into an office after the baptism of fire known as the interview. It's an old, old custom, recently refined and extended by many. A hundred years ago, all we needed was a good reference, a deferential manner, a little white paint on our shirt cuffs and some boot blacking on hair and jacket elbows. Now we may be subjected to a day or more of meetings and tours round the office and tests of physical, mental and moral aptitude.

But the form of the interview and its purpose remains the same – to discover whether or not the candidate is the right person for the job. This includes an examination as to how well the candidate will fit in with current office staff and practice. At its best, the interview is a two-way process. Both sides are on trial. With around three million unemployed, it may be that the interviewee has the most to lose, but that shouldn't mean that those conducting the interview may behave in a high-handed fashion. Any employer wants the best possible recruit to the staff. It would be a grave mistake to have the ideal applicant turn down a job because the interviewers were rude or thoughtless.

13

Conducting an interview

Thought should always be given as to how an interview is to be conducted. There are a lot of questions that need to be answered. How many people should be on the panel? Who should be in charge? How long should the interview last? What's the prime purpose of the interview? How should the seating be arranged? How should each candidate be greeted? What sort of refreshments, if any, should be served, by whom and when? What sort of time should be allotted for the candidates to ask their own questions, and who is to decide which member of the panel should respond to such questions?

Most offices have long established their own procedures, but it doesn't hurt to run a regular checklist over the tried, and possibly tired, format. And it shouldn't be necessary to remind those holding an interview that if it has to be cancelled or postponed for any reason, candidates should be told as soon as possible.

If only one person is conducting the interview, then there is no problem as to who's in charge or how many should be on the panel. But thought needs to be given to where the interview should take place, and how the seating should be arranged. The interview room should be clean and tidy; business-like, giving the sort of impression that the company wishes to project. It's not a good idea to interview someone in a corridor or in a couple of chairs in a corner of the reception area. It suggests that the interview is a nuisance, a half-forgotten piece of trivia that's getting in the way of what really matters. On the other hand, an interview conducted in a conference chamber the size of the concourse at Paddington Station is hardly likely to put the candidate at ease and allow him or her to give of their best. If it's a one-to-one interview, then it should take place in the interviewer's own office, probably with the two parties sitting on opposite sides of the desk, though some prefer a more side-by-side approach. If the candidate is to be interviewed by a panel, then the choice is an open one. Some prefer the panel to sit behind a table or tables (arranged in an inverted U-shape if there are lots of people

14

interviewing), others prefer a circle of chairs. It isn't fair, and it's bad manners, to make candidates face interviewers who are sitting with their backs to windows or other sources of light, so that all the candidates see is a series of silhouettes. Not only is it bad manners, it's inefficient (as are most examples of bad manners) because it prevents candidates performing to the best of their abilities, and the company may therefore turn down someone they should have taken.

Whatever layout is decided upon, it should be clear who is in charge. The candidate will have been already welcomed by the receptionist on arrival, and probably by the chairperson's secretary subsequently. Unless the candidate has been unlucky or silly, he or she will have arrived in good time to relax a little and go to the loo if need be. At the appointed hour for the interview, the chair of the interviewing panel should appear on the scene and make the necessary introductions. The candidate should be gently ushered into the room where the interview will take place, introduced to the rest of the panel (slowly, because it takes a long time to register who's who – and don't bother at all if the panel's a large one), and shown where to sit. Little of this should take the candidate by surprise. Some indication as to the size and make-up of the panel should have been already communicated by phone or letter.

Asking questions
The chairperson should open proceedings by making the candidate feel welcome (again), asking if he or she had a good journey, thanking them for coming, saying how pleased the company is to meet them. The next thing is to outline how the interview will be conducted, what its purpose is, roughly how long it will last, and what time will be set aside for the candidate to ask questions of the panel. After this, the questions begin.

There are hundreds of questions that may be asked at interview: there are one or two that shouldn't be. It is fair enough to ask candidates questions about their previous work records and experiences, about any problems they might have travelling to the job, about their career ambitions, etc. It is not acceptable to ask questions about their political allegiances (even if an attempt is made to hide this by asking what newspaper the candidate reads), religious beliefs, or breeding intentions. If candidates are asked such questions, they have to edge their ways diplomatically round them – more on this later in the chapter – but those asking such questions lose a great many points and may well be breaking the law.

The way in which these questions are asked will set the whole tone of the interview. If the questions are too forceful, then there is the danger that the interview will deteriorate into an argument. If they're not forceful enough, little will be discovered about the candidates. Good interview questions are open-ended, they allow the candidates chances to speak at some length. 'Do you think you would be good at this job?' is not as helpful a question as 'How do you see yourself in this job?' Apart from the obvious fact that no candidate is going to answer 'No' to the first question, it doesn't ellicit information, it doesn't draw the candidate out, it doesn't invite a whole range of answers from a range of candidates – and that's what is needed for the panel to make a decision.

Refreshments can pose problems at interviews. If coffee or tea is served halfway through the interview, it breaks the flow of the meeting. If it's served at the end, the whole thing becomes an uncomfortable tea party. Better to give the candidate a cup of tea or coffee on arrival – if there's time – so that they can get it out of their way. Nobody is at their best balancing a cup on their knee, munching a biscuit and trying to answer questions intelligently at the same time. And coffee, tea, fruit juice or mineral water are the only liquids that should be offered. An interview is not the right setting for a booze-up.

At the end of the interview, the candidates should be asked if there are any questions they wish to ask. When it's clear that these have been dealt with (or when the panel justifiably feel they have had enough), the interview should be brought to an end by the chairperson. Each candidate is again thanked for attending, and it should be made clear when and how they will be informed of the outcome of their application. If the office is a large one, each candidate should be given clear directions as to how to get out, so that they can rush into the nearest pub to drown their sorrows or race into the nearest store to buy themselves a present for having done so well.

How the interviewee should behave
The first thing for any candidate to do is to respond to the invitation to the interview – i.e. to let people know that he or she will attend or can't attend. The second thing is to arrive at the right place at the right time on the right day. Strange how such a simple task should so often present major difficulties. The trouble is that trains are often late, roads are often blocked, cars often break down – so none of these excuses is impressive, and none of them brings any real sympathy, whatever is said. So we should always set out in good time, catch a train earlier than the one that will get there in time, assume an average speed far slower than that hoped for on the road. If something disastrous happens, something way beyond our control, and we know we are going to be late, then we should communicate this information to our interviewers as soon and as politely as possible.

The third thing is to present ourselves to our best advantage. We shouldn't turn up looking sloppy or crumpled or ill-dressed. If we go to the loo on arrival at the place of interview, we should check our dress afterwards – people have found it very difficult to do up a zip unobserved during an interview. We should also always take a supply of paper handkerchiefs with us when we set off for an interview. We shouldn't be rude or give the impression that turning up for this blessed business is the last thing we wanted. We should take notice of who and what is around us. Smiling (politely, no leers or lecherous grins, please) at the receptionist, doorman, and any staff who greet us, always helps. They sometimes smile back. On arrival we state who we are and

17

whom we have come to see. From then on we should merely have to react to the appropriate cues and questions that we are given.

At the interview itself it's unwise to assume that we should adopt the tone of the panel. There may be a catch in this – they may be giving the impression of riotous familiarity to test us out. It's best to be polite, but not ingratiatingly so. If we are nervous that may well be apparent. In extremis we may mention that we are nervous, though that may not necessarily make us feel any more comfortable. Questions should be answered as directly as possible – experienced panels and interviewers have a built-in radar for recognising flannel. If we don't understand a question, we should say so, and ask for it to be repeated, or rephrased or explained. At an interview where I didn't understand one of the terms used, I asked the questioner to say what he meant. He refused, and repeated the question. So I prefaced my answer by giving my definition of the term used, and answering the question in the light of that definition. No harm was done, apparently – I got the job.

We should save our own questions for the end of the interview unless invited to state them earlier. It's quite permissible to ask about salary, conditions of employment, whether there's a staff canteen, etc. etc. It isn't a good idea to ask if we can have the first two weeks off in June before we've even been offered the job. When it's clear that the interview is over, we should thank the panel generally, and the chairperson in particular, and then leave. If they don't tell us when and how we'll hear the result of the interview, it does no harm to ask. Stories are told of interviewees who turn at the door and say 'Look, I know you're not going to offer me the job, but could you tell me why?' and who then get the job. Into every life a little luck must fall, but the question runs the risk of getting a brusque answer. It should only be posed if we see ourselves as very strong candidates who didn't do ourselves justice, *and who know exactly why and how we didn't do ourselves justice.*

18

After the interview

If we have already shown that we are polite, it is acceptable to write a follow-up letter after the interview, thanking the chair and the panel for their time and hospitality. We shouldn't make such a letter seem unctuous. If we are offered the job (and we still want it), we should write to accept at once – this is the business world we are dealing with, no points are gained by showing cool restraint or trying to suggest that we're so busy that we've hardly time to acknowledge their important communication. If we don't want the job, we should have already phoned or, better, written to the company to tell them. Indeed, if we become totally, utterly and irrefutably convinced we don't want the job during the interview, we should say so there and then.

Similarly, the chairperson or whoever conducted the interview should write to all candidates after a decision has been made or earlier if that decision is likely to be delayed. It's extremely bad manners to leave candidates to assume that they haven't got the job simply because they haven't heard anything and several weeks have passed. And, who knows, one day one of those unsuccessful candidates may be in a position to become a valued customer.

If we didn't get the job, it is permissible to write (not phone) and ask if we could be given reasons why we didn't. We may not like the reply, but there's no harm in asking. We cannot, however, then enter into a correspondence along the lines of 'well, I'm a sight better than she is/you'll live to regret it/the whole thing's a fix.' No company has to justify its decision in giving a job to one candidate rather than another, but it isn't unreasonable for an unsuccessful candidate to want to know what went wrong with their own application. Once we've been given that reason, the matter is closed.

Body language

In the wonderfully sophisticated age in which we live, more and more people are becoming aware of the science of body language. It now matters how we sit, what we do with our legs and arms and hands, and even how we walk into an interview. Crossed arms indicates a defensive attitude. Hands in trouser pockets is still considered impolite by many in the case of men, and one hand nonchalantly thrust into her jacket pocket by a woman is considered by some to indicate arrogance. Legs may be crossed, but not ostentatiously so, and not if such action reveals a stretch of white flesh above the sock top in the case of men, or too much stockinged leg in the case of women. Neither men nor women should attempt to flirt with an interviewer – if it helps get the job, so much the worse for that company. It's a bit like Groucho Marx's remark about not wanting to pay ten dollars to join a club that admits people like him.

The face should be left alone during the interview. Pulling on the earlobe, *à la* Humphrey Bogart, may not lose points; picking the teeth or nose, or fussing with the hairstyle invariably will. If we have to blow our nose, there's no harm in that, so we shouldn't try to do it furtively. At the same time, there's no need to make a meal of it. The hands should be as still as possible, though it's quite all right to gesticulate to add emphasis to what we are saying. What has to be avoided is waving them about meaninglessly, or fidgeting with the fingers. This can be distracting for the interviewers and interfere with their concentration on what we are saying. In extreme cases it may make them think that they are dealing with a neurotic. If we are really uncomfortable, we should say so. Maybe there's something wrong with the chair, or we're suddenly feeling ill. Better to ask for another hearing or a break in the proceedings if we feel we're performing way below potential because we're not well. If we need to go to the loo – well, we should have gone when we arrived – but we have to say so. Better that, than leaving the interviewers to guess.

Smoking at interviews
The general rule is that nobody should smoke at an interview. If the interview is going to last more than a couple of hours,

then a break should be built into the schedule – a time when whoever needs to smoke may go to a designated smoking area and do so. If the interview lasts less than two hours – and most do – then a No Smoking rule should be enforced. If an interviewer lights up, this is bad manners. If an interviewee lights up, this is bad manners and is going to prejudice chances of success. If members of the interview panel are smoking, and a candidate has a chronic need to follow suit, then he or she should ask first. This is a delicate matter, for by asking it may seem that the candidate is indirectly drawing attention to the bad manners of the panel who are already smoking. This is why, if smoking has to be allowed at the interview, the chairperson should make that known to everyone (including the interviewee) at the outset of the meeting by announcing: 'This is going to be a meeting at which it will be acceptable to smoke if no one has any strong objections.' A bold candidate may raise objections – the timid among us suffer in smoke-filled silence.

It's better all round if the chairperson makes it clear that smoking will not be allowed, and nobody smokes.

CHECKLIST

1. Companies should regularly review their interview systems and techniques.
2. The purpose of an interview should be to get the best out of a candidate.
3. One person should clearly be in charge of an interview.
4. The board sets the tone of the interview: the candidate's responsibility is to pick this up and run with it.
5. Candidates must be punctual.
6. Candidates must dress appropriately – a little homework may be necessary here.
7. A follow-up letter to the chairperson of the interview, thanking him or her, is often a politic move.
8. It isn't only what we say in an interview that matters, it is how we say it, and how we sit while we are saying it.

9. Never smoke at an interview unless invited to.
10. Don't burn bridges. Storming out hurling insults when we didn't get the job will do irreparable harm to our chances of being interviewed for another job with the same company. And if they have contacts with other companies in the same line of business . . .

CHAPTER 3

Getting settled

Each venture
Is a new beginning, a raid on the inarticulate
With shabby equipment always deteriorating
In the general mess of imprecision of feeling
T.S. ELIOT – *East Coker*

The interviews have been held. The choice has been made. The joyous day arrives when the new appointee enters the office to start work there for the first time. Early impressions are important for both the newcomer and those already well settled into the practices and routines of this particular office. It isn't a time to reveal petty office squabbles and jealousies, and to try to recruit the newcomer into one gang or clique. It isn't a time for either party or either sex to make passionate advances. It isn't a time for either the newcomer or the old sweats to suggest that the respective performances at the interview were merely false fronts, and that neither side has the remotest interest in being a conscientious worker.

How the newcomer should be inducted
The company should have a well established policy and framework for introducing new staff to the workplace. This applies at all levels. The first few days are as difficult and stressful for the new receptionist as they are for the new managing director. Whoever is starting work should have someone deputed to look after them, to introduce them to their new colleagues, and generally to show them the ropes.

This person should have been informed when the newcomer was starting, and should then have made arrangements to be informed of the newcomer's arrival. It doesn't hurt to show a little concern by asking the newcomer how the journey was, and then it's down to work. A conducted tour is essential – no-one should have to work out for themselves where the loos are, where the canteen is, where the stairs, lifts and emergency exits are. The newcomer should be accompanied to his or her place of work, and introduced to those with whom he or she will be working most closely. These introductions should be as formal or informal as the ethos of the workplace allows. If the general practice is to call people by their first names, then the introductions can include first names: 'Vernon Friley, this is Ivy Benson, our chief cashier/director of accounts/whatever.' The newcomer is introduced to the old hand. Sometimes, the old hands may prefer to make their own introductions: 'I'm Janette . . . Janette Scott, Head of Sales and Marketing.' The way these introductions are made should indicate whether first or family names are to be used. If they don't, then the person with responsibility for showing the newcomer around should say what the office practice is with regard to names, and, anyway, should alert the newcomer to any mavericks who don't like to fit in with the general practice.

The newcomer should be shown where he or she will work. This should be more than a simple: 'That's your desk over there.' Anyone starting in a new workplace needs a lot of information about such matters as phones, office hours, lunch and tea breaks, stationery, health and safety, word processors, filing cabinets, who to go to for what, and a great deal more.

Phones

Better not to assume that everyone is as honest as the driven snow and will never make a private call on the company's phone. Better to say what the rules are regarding the phone. If private calls aren't allowed, say so; if local private calls are allowed, say so; if private calls are allowed if it's an emergency, or if it's to a wife, husband or partner, say so – otherwise there is always the risk of an unpleasant little recriminatory meeting later, full of 'I didn't knows' and

'Nobody told mes' and 'Well, you must have thoughts'.

In the interest of efficiency, it also helps if the newcomer knows how the phone system works, how to make internal and external calls, whether the calls go through a switchboard, and if there are any special ways the company has of saving money on the phone – e.g. pointing out that international calls will be cheaper if made outside peak hours.

Office hours

This sort of information should have been given to the newcomer at interview. It doesn't hurt to repeat it on the first day. No employer should assume that a newcomer knows what the office practice is with regard to working hours. Often this is not a clear matter. It may be that someone is employed to work set hours, the traditional 9 to 5, Monday to Friday, with perhaps some weekend work spasmodically. More and more, however, people are expected to work the hours that it takes to do their job. This tends to be interpreted by companies as meaning that the hours of work may regularly stretch beyond 5 p.m., rather than that employees may disappear in mid-afternoon.

How to behave as a newcomer

Any change in the pattern of life is tiring and stressful, whether it's moving house, breaking up with a partner or changing jobs. Few are at their best socially at such a time. This is why consideration needs to be shown to any new recruit to a company. At the same time, the new recruit has to make sure that exhaustion and bewilderment aren't likely to be interpreted as distant, uninterested, snooty or insensitive behaviour.

Working in a new office means there is a lot to be learned. Everyone takes time to adjust. There are new names to be put to new faces, new routines and new systems to be assimilated, and there's a new ethos to which the newcomer has to adapt. The problem is that, while ignorance is acceptable for a while in this situation, incompetence and impoliteness aren't. It's perfectly forgivable to forget where the paper clips are kept, less so not to remember the immediate superior's name or title. But what most of the rest of the office staff are looking at (and doubtless quietly commenting upon to each other), is how well or badly the new recruit 'fits in'.

Fitting in

Unless there are very good reasons for doing otherwise, there's a lot to be said for following the old advice 'When in Rome do as the Romans do'. If the general tone of the office is quiet and reserved, then overtures of extreme mateyness on the part of the newcomer will be out of place and unwelcome. Some people get into the habit of picking up the nearest phone or sitting at the nearest computer, regardless of whose it is. If this has been the past practice of the newcomer, he or she shouldn't assume that it may be imported into the new workplace. The human race is still very animalistic when it comes to the protection of private space and property. Many of us remember bitterly and to the grave those who have borrowed pens, books, lawnmowers, torches and screwdrivers and never returned them. So, if the general impression is that staff in the office keep themselves very much to themselves, then this has to be respected, *even if it doesn't seem the right way to work*. No matter how much the newcomer itches to make improvements, he or she has initially to exercise profound self-control.

Similarly, if the office buzzes with merry chatter and banter, then an unyieldingly frigid response to every overture of friendship isn't appropriate. Most workplaces have a detectable *esprit de bureau*, covering such diverse questions as whether or not everyone is expected to attend the office party, to meet informally after work on Friday to unwind, to support other colleagues if they're deluged with work, to cover for absences, to take part in social awaydays, etc. The newcomer ignores this at his or her peril. There has to be some measure of compromise in almost all human activity. Leading colleagues to new and improved ways of working is something

26

better done later rather than sooner.

The likelihood is, of course, that the personnel of any office constitute a mixed bunch. Some will keep themselves much to themselves, others will be insatiably nosy, many will take up a position somewhere between these two extremes. There will be those who never progress beyond a polite 'Good morning' at 9 a.m., and a polite 'Goodnight' at 5 p.m. There will be those on Day One who wish to initiate the new recruit into the ways of the League for the Promulgation of Office Gossip, and reveal all about office Lotharios, alcoholics, and eccentrics. The former present no real problem: the latter can rapidly become a pain in the neck. The best way to handle the former is to be polite. The best way to handle the latter is, firstly, never to join in the gossip or suggest that it's fascinating; secondly, to show that there are other, more important things to do; and, thirdly (if the gossipmongers persist), politely but firmly to indicate that their behaviour is neither helpful nor appropriate. If this produces a backlash of resentment (it almost certainly will), then the firm but polite front has to be maintained until the gossipmongers latch on to someone else and/or realise that it's possible to co-exist without being fellow conspirators in some illicit practice.

What if it all gets too much?
To complain is not to behave badly. For more on this un-English approach to life's problems, see Chapter 11.

Who to turn to for help
One of the things that should have been made clear when the newcomer was introduced to the office is where and from whom advice is obtainable – 'If you have any queries, see so-and-so . . .' or 'Don't hesitate to come to me if there's anything you don't understand . . .' There are reasons why certain people are indicated as potential sources of help.

They may have expertise. Quite possibly, it's their job to

help or they may have special responsibility for assisting newcomers. If there are problems, difficulties, or matters that don't make sense, the correct thing to do is follow the advice given and go to the person mentioned. Going to other people is inadvisable for two reasons:

1. They may give the wrong advice, and
2. It suggests a willingness to ignore suggested procedures.

The general rule is to accept the system as it is presented, even if there seem to be short cuts. Tinkering with the system and improving it can come later, when the newcomer has grown into an experienced old hand.

If no one has been indicated as the person to turn to for help, the newcomer should go to his or her immediate superior or whoever has taken on the role of pastoral care.

Pushing new ideas
A newcomer may be bursting to communicate how much better he or she handled matters at the previous workplace. There are few things worse than the daily frustration of knowing that it's possible to work faster and more efficiently but not being allowed to do so. Tact is needed here. Whizz-kids may act as though it isn't and may charge in saying 'Let me show you how we did this at Noble and Bowlly's', but the whizz-kid image is one that takes a lot of living up to, and whizz-kids don't make many friends. Again it's a matter of going to the right person (whoever has the authority to implement such changes) and starting up a conversation along the lines of 'I wonder if it would be a good idea if we . . .' or 'what if we were to . . .' It's also not a bad idea to have a memo prepared on the subject, in case the person to whom this brilliant new idea is entrusted tries to steal it.

Once the newcomer has graduated to old hand, the brilliant and innovative ideas can flow like a river in spate.

Taking on new staff

There are two elements in the way a newcomer is received in an office – the formal and the informal.

The formal element is the responsibility of whoever has been given the task of looking after the new recruit. This may include:

1. Greeting the newcomer on arrival for the first day's work (see earlier this chapter).
2. Generally keeping an eye out and checking that all is well for the first week or two.
3. Introducing the newcomer to his or her colleagues.
4. Explaining to the newcomer how the office works and what procedures exist if things go wrong.
5. Preparing the way for things to go right.

It's not a bad idea to book a meeting with the newcomer a few weeks ahead to review how things are going. It gives the newcomer something to hold on to, and avoids the possibility of minor difficulties turning into major problems. It also shows a degree of concern.

The informal element is more complex in that it is the joint and sum responsibility of everyone in the office, and there will be a hotch-potch of approaches and attitudes to the newcomer. What is most needed is sensitivity and consideration on these points:

1. Bombarded with new names and new titles in a new environment, the newcomer may justifiably forget who's who and what they do.
2. Even the brightest and best may not find unfamiliar office machinery user-friendly from Day One.
3. Overcome with anxiety, they may momentarily fail to say 'please' and 'thank you' when they should.
4. A preoccupied mind isn't always conscious of the hand of friendship.
5. Everyone needs space in their lives.

6. Mistakes are easily and innocently made.

If a newcomer seeks help, it should be given willingly, ungrudgingly and unpatronisingly. If a newcomer is clearly floundering but hasn't sought help (for whatever reason – shyness or foolish pride), it is both polite and appropriate to ask if they would like some help. If a newcomer is making clear mistakes, the right thing to do is to show them how not to, rather than to take the matter out of their hands, or to sit back, fold the arms and let a smile of superiority slide over the face. Everyone in an office has a great deal to do, and it takes longer for a newcomer to do even the most humdrum of tasks. Once the newcomer has learnt who everyone is and where everything is, he or she will raise the level of performance. Being invited to take part in even the most informal lunchtime or after-hours gatherings can be tiring and bewildering to a newcomer – they should always be invited, but declining an invitation or failing to turn up having accepted one doesn't necessarily indicate rudeness. A great many people go through their professional life wishing to be neither friends nor enemies of everyone. The strengths of their predecessor in the post may not be fascinating to a newcomer. The weaknesses of their predecessor in the post almost certainly will be. An occasionally uttered 'How are things?' can be a helpful way in for a newcomer to voice whatever they're unsure of or worried about. If their response is a two-hour moan about everything and everybody (including their lover's lack of personal hygiene and the failure of the United Nations to solve a couple of dozen global problems), well, an important lesson has been learnt and the question need never be uttered again.

CHECKLIST

1. It helps if there is someone within the company with the responsibility to welcome and introduce newcomers.
2. Guidance should be given to newcomers on the degree of formality or informality within the office.

3. Much time is saved if newcomers are shown where phones, faxes, and photocopiers, etc. are to be found.
4. It should be made clear at the outset what is expected of a newcomer in terms of hours of work and duties.
5. Patience needs to be exercised by newcomer and old stagers during the probationary first week or two.
6. Newcomers should be sensitive to the prevailing office atmosphere.
7. Newcomers should beware the office gossips and malcontents.
8. Asking for help or clarification is not a sign of weakness.
9. Both sides may benefit from a fixed review of how things are going a few weeks after starting.
10. What matters is not how many mistakes a newcomer makes, but how quickly he or she learns from them.

CHAPTER 4

Formal Introductions

I wish I loved the Human Race;
I wish I loved its silly face;
I wish I liked the way it walks;
I wish I liked the way it talks;
And when I'm introduced to one
I wish I thought *What Jolly Fun*!
SIR WALTER RALEIGH –
Laughter from a Cloud
(no, a different
Sir Walter Raleigh, d. 1922)

Most of us have a great deal to learn from the French in the art of how people should be introduced to each other. They seem to know instinctively who is presented to whom, whether to shake hands or kiss, how many kisses should be given (and which cheek to start with), and how gently or firmly to press (rather than shake) a hand. They have educated their entire population in this skill. I was cycling through Normandy one summer when I had to stop at a temporary traffic light by some road works. A gang of eight men were digging up the road. A small van drew up, and another workman got out. He went up to the eight, and solemnly greeted each one of them – each in turn put down pick or shovel, wiped hand on trousers, shook hands, and then picked up pick or shovel. The whole operation lasted nearly ten minutes, and I was grateful for the rest.

In Britain, there have been articles written about The Art of Shaking Hands. People rehearse in their minds how to do it, worry about damp palms, reflect on how firm the handshake should be in terms of lbs pressure per digit. It's a

33

wonder some bright entrepreneur hasn't thought of running weekend courses on the subject or marketing a Handshake Video.

A handshake, we are told, should be firm but not crippling. It should neither crush bones nor resemble caressing a piece of wet fish. The right sort of handshake shows 'character'. The wrong sort reveals 'deficiencies'. It may do, it may not. But it does seem true to say that the consensus of opinion in Britain is that a handshake should be firm, dry and of not too long a duration.

It is given with the right hand, unless one is greeting a fellow Scout, and usually without bringing the left hand down on top of the entwined right hands – though there's nothing illegal about this somewhat American enhancement. It is the correct way to greet colleagues, clients, customers, diplomats, digna-tories and even Her Majesty, provided she shows willing by proffering her hand first.

It is also now the almost universal method of greeting (see separate chapters in Part Two for variations on the theme).

Greeting with a kiss
Within the framework of business etiquette, the general rule is 'don't'. Of course, if a client or colleague is also a friend, that's a different matter, but otherwise it should never be assumed that even a gentle kiss is acceptable. Like all general rules, this has exceptions, the most obvious being when in France. If everyone else in the party is busily pecking *à gauche, à droit* regardless of status, familiarity or nationality, then it's not only safe to join in, but probably politic as well. A safe fallback rule is 'if in doubt, don't'.

How to introduce people
It may help to commit one or two simple rules to memory here. All else being equal, the Three Commandments are:

1. Introduce juniors to seniors ('Mr Goodman, may I present/introduce Tommy Dorsey? Mr Goodman is our

Senior Vice President. Tommy is one of our part-time researchers . . .').

2. Introduce men to women ('Ms Day, this is Mr Shaw, our Staff Liaison Officer. Ms Day is Mr Herman's new Personal Assistant . . .').
3. Introduce colleagues to clients ('Mr Ellington, I'd like you to meet Mr Basie. Bill Basie is a key member of our sales team. Bill, Mr Ellington is interested in our new 12 octave keyboard . . .').

There is no need to wave the hands to and fro or continually nod the head during this process, but most people do. Grabbing those being introduced by the wrist or shoulder in an effort to bring them physically closer to each other is not a good idea unless we are in dear-old-pals territory and are about to follow up the more formal introduction with a line such as 'I know you two are going to get on famously . . .' – usually a dreadful mistake.

What matters far more than any theatrical gestures is that the verbal introductions are delivered in a clear voice and at a reasonable speed. The aim of the whole process is not to show how matey we all are or that the person making the introductions should be running his or her own TV chat show, but to enable two strangers to learn each other's names and roles.

'I'm sorry, I didn't quite catch . . .'
The business world is not a place for faint hearts. There are dozens of occasions when even the shyest among us has to take a deep breath and break into a conversation. One of these occasions is when we have been introduced to someone and we simply didn't manage to catch the name. It happens over and over again, and yet many people try to bluff their way through it, hoping that the name will be repeated naturally in the conversation soon. And then, the person who made the introductions says 'Well, I'll leave you two to it' and trots off, and within seconds a third party comes along whom we ought to introduce to our now nameless companion.

35

It is quite permissible to ask for a name or title to be repeated, and even, if it's a complicated or unusual name that we still haven't grasped, to ask for it to be spelt out. Better to show a genuine concern to learn someone's name than to act as though it isn't worth committing to memory.

Special people
There are more complicated rules about how to introduce special people – those of rank or official standing. It doesn't happen all the time, but it is not unknown in the business world to come across ambassadors, princes, ministers or aristocrats. For the ambitious among us, there are books packed with advice on how to deal with such situations, including how to make formal introductions. The best thing to do is buy one or ask for a coaching session with the firm's Court Correspondent.

CHECKLIST

1. Being too formal is probably better than being too informal.
2. Seniors are introduced to juniors.
3. Men are introduced to women.
4. Colleagues are introduced to clients.
5. The purpose of introductions is to allow people to learn each other's names and professional roles.
6. It is permissible to ask for a name to be repeated.
7. To avoid the need for repetition, introductions should be made in a clear voice.
8. When being introduced, we should adopt a friendly demeanour, but not a nauseatingly ingratiating one.
9. Special rules apply when introducing special people. These need to be consulted separately.
10. Special rules apply in other cultures – see Part Two of this book.

CHAPTER 5

Office Organisation

There are only two qualities in the world: efficiency and inefficiency, and only two sorts of people: the efficient and the inefficient.

GEORGE BERNARD SHAW – *John Bull's Other Island*

The image of office life projected by Hollywood (*Wall Street; Glengarry Glen Ross*) is of a cut-throat world where the Good Samaritan would get his cards by lunchtime on Day One for failing to meet sales targets. It's a mistake to assume, however, that bad manners or inconsiderate behaviour helps to pull in those prized orders from the home or export market. Hollywood spins fine stories: it doesn't always reflect reality. People work better when they are content. People feel content when they feel that they are appreciated and that they have been given a chance to contribute. People feel they are appreciated when they are treated with politeness.

Part of the job of any office manager should be to make sure that people feel at ease with each other, that there is some kind of team spirit at work, that there is mutual respect. It may be that everyone has quite enough to do without having to spend time throwing up their hands in delighted admiration at the way a colleague has completed a spreadsheet or sent a fax to Australia, so we are not so much looking for a list of dos here, as don'ts.

Neither a borrower, a thief, nor a squatter be . . .

1. Don't use other people's desks as temporary (or permanent) dumping grounds for files, folders, newspapers,

empty coffee mugs, raincoats, sandwiches or (worst!) cigarette ends.

2. Don't think an icy stare and a grimly muttered 'Uh' is an adequate substitute for a reasonably pleasant 'Good morning' (never mind about the smile – that may come later and we can't expect miracles).

3. Don't lean over to a neighbouring desk to pinch pens, envelopes, sticky labels, an *A to Z*, or (worst!) a stapler when there aren't any on your own.

4. Don't expect someone else always to make the tea, water the plants, put new toilet rolls in the staff loos, or (worst!) wash the mugs unless it is their job to do this.

5. Don't expect someone else to answer the phone that's ringing on an unoccupied desk.

6. Don't assume that it's permissible to smoke just because no-one's said it isn't and there aren't any 'No Smoking' signs about (more on this later).

7. If you do answer the unattended phone, don't doodle on the paper beside it (more on the etiquette of the telephone in Chapter 16).

8. Don't suggest that whatever anyone else is doing or talking about must be of secondary importance by cutting across their conversations.

9. Don't adopt a sliding scale of behaviour, starting with hand-licking servility to the office manager and ending with haughty arrogance towards the junior typist.

10. Don't assume that employment as (say) Transport Manager means that it would be wrong to open the door for a colleague or help to carry boxes of stationery across the room.

Team work

Even if not formally constituted as such, most office staffs are supposed to work as a team. This is defined in the OED as 'a number of persons associated in some joint action'. It's the 'joint action' part of the definition that matters here. Some conscientious Sales Manager may sweat for days in negotiations with hard-nosed clients to gain a prestigious contract. Some timid young lad may put the toner in the photocopier so that copies of this wonderful contract may be printed and sent hither and thither. The Sales Manager may be earning £10,000 a month: the young lad may be earning £10,000 a year. Both are part of a team, and that should regularly (if not always) be recognised. Here are some of the ways in which the existence of the team is often ignored:

1. No appreciation is given of the fact that a subordinate often has to reschedule all his or her work to meet the demands of a senior. The obvious example is of a boss who spends all day preparing a report and then expects the secretary to spend all evening typing it up and photocopying it. The logistics may be unavoidable. The assumption that the secretary needs no special thanks or appreciation isn't.

2. Credit is not fairly shared for something going right.

3. Little or no importance is attached to what other people are doing. This often manifests itself in the 'There was some sort of telephone message for you while you were out, but I haven't the slightest idea who it was or what it was about . . .' syndrome.

4. People keep very quiet when volunteers are called for to organise some social occasion or take on responsibilities for the office party, on the grounds that 'Old Ambrose always does that . . .'

5. There is a lack of preparedness to come to the aid of a colleague who has made a complete mess of his or her appointments schedule, or who is having to deal with two traumatic phone calls at the same time, or who clearly ought to go straight home having been suddenly smitten with the flu.

6. Colleagues, particularly junior colleagues, are given orders rather than instructions – i.e. words of command are hurled over the shoulder or thrown on the desk as the senior sweeps by.

7. An important document goes missing (it happens) and the sole concern of the entire office is 'who is to blame?', not 'where might the document be?', or 'is there another copy?'
8. Something has gone right, and nobody wants to share out any of the credit for it.
9. Some members of staff spend much effort in noting how much time other members of staff waste, without noting the amount of time they are themselves wasting on this process.
10. Members of staff gain an unhealthy nourishment from frequently repeating to themselves such phrases as 'Nobody works harder for this firm than I do . . .'

Assembling the team, creating the atmosphere
It is almost impossible for a team spirit to be fostered from the bottom upwards. News of this fact may come as a great relief to office managers and chief executives, who too often view junior initiatives as heralding a Bolshevik revival, but managing a team is a lot easier than quelling a riot, which is in turn easier than having to do everything oneself. Pretty speeches and far-flung memos have limited effectiveness in assembling a team. Personal example is what is needed, along the lines of:

1. Good manners at all times – opening doors for those with their hands full, whoever they may be; holding the lift doors open for those who would otherwise just miss it; greeting everyone at least civilly; showing respect in the way people are addressed.
2. Giving credit where credit is due, and letting it be known that this has been done.
3. Giving as much notice as possible of the looming danger of extra hours having to be worked.
4. Showing sufficient interest in colleagues to note when one of them seems ill, worried, under stress, confused or in any other way impaired.
5. Communicating good news or appreciation from on

high to everyone concerned, rather than hogging it to oneself.

6. Scotching rumour or gossip or tittle-tattle – all of which will eventually have a negative effect on morale and leave a nasty taste in the mouth, however piquant it may seem at the time.
7. Consulting people before decisions are made – especially those which will directly concern them.
8. Listening to what people have to say, rather than giving the impression that there really isn't time.
9. Encouraging people to work together where appropriate.
10. Generally behaving as though a team exists.

All this is largely, if not entirely, a matter of common sense. The problem comes not only in assembling a team but in keeping it going. A team doesn't have the permanence of, say, the Black Mountains or the movement of the oceans. Once assembled it has to be constantly nourished, the more so since its composition may regularly change. Good managers keep mental or written checklists of what they should do to provide this nourishment. When I was Head of an inner city school, we were sent by our local authority a booklet that contained a list of valuable questions about management techniques. We were asked to check how often we spoke to various members of the school population, including school caretakers, dinner ladies, school crossing attendants, classroom assistants, parents and the children themselves. Failure to give people a chance to talk about their work will almost invariably lead to their feeling a lack of appreciation, however lofty their position in the hierarchy of the company.

Perhaps it's simply a matter of recognising that talkers are ten a penny, listeners are as rare as old groats.

Empty words or the real intent?
Just as democracy isn't achieved merely by voting once every five years in a General Election, so good office organisation

41

shouldn't stop short at designing a structure and writing a checklist. Responsibility has to be taken for monitoring what is happening, or initially, for introducing any changes in how the office is to be run. The extent to which a sense of teamwork is established and a pleasant atmosphere created will depend on the sensitivity shown by management.

Management should be receptive to and appreciative of new ideas from junior members of staff, whether these ideas are good or bad, old or new, commercial or social. The 'we'll tell you what's best for you' approach has long been ripe for burial. Anyone who thinks they have a way of making office life better or of ensuring a rosy financial future for the company should be listened to with respect. Clearly, not everyone is in a position to listen to new ideas all day every day. There are, therefore, good and not-so-good ways of presenting the fruits of genius:

1. Make sure that the idea is coherent, and not half-baked.
2. Check that it is relevant, new and constructive.
3. Give thought to how best to present it – a little rehearsal can help.
4. Select the correct person to present it to.
5. Make an appointment to see this person and give some brief idea of what will be on the agenda when this meeting takes place.
6. If there is a need to, take steps to protect the idea from poachers.
7. Turn up at the appointed hour and present the idea clearly and concisely.
8. Be appreciative of the time given to do so.
9. Listen to what response is made. If the new idea seems to pass the first hurdle, ask what happens next.
10. Make sure credit is given to any colleagues who have been party to the new idea.

The surprised, shocked, delighted, appalled or bored recipient of the new idea should respond correctly:

1. Show that he or she welcomes the opportunity to listen to the budding office genius.
2. Encourage the genius in the presentation of the idea.
3. Without committing superiors in any way, acknowledge that the idea is a good idea, if it *is* a good idea.
4. Gently dissuade (rather than insult) the genius if it isn't a good idea.
5. Avoid rash or unrealistic promises.
6. Carry out whatever promises are made to further the progress of the idea (nothing dispirits a work force more than empty promises, whether they're about pay rises, security of employment, better work conditions or whatever).
7. Be honest about where the idea came from if superiors love it.
8. Avoid the temptation of initiating a character assassination of the genius if superiors don't fall in love with the new idea.
9. Seek to involve as many people as possible in sharing the good news if the idea is a success.
10. Avoid the temptation to use one person's success as a stick with which to beat the rest of the office staff who haven't come up with a good idea.

Which leads to:

Acknowledgement of work and success
Most planning and structuring in all walks of life is about avoiding accidents and mistakes, disciplining wrong-doers, preventing people getting away with anything from murder to pinching a roll of loo paper from the staff toilet – in short, the negative things in life. Laws are all about wrongdoing. Few of us spend sufficient (or indeed any) time trying to work out how best to legislate for good things, how to construct a framework so that we may properly reward success and honest

43

endeavour. It's a pity and a mistake. Those who deserve praise and don't get it have a habit of disappearing and joining rival companies, football teams, television shows; and by then it's too late to acknowledge their value. And this doesn't apply solely to ace researchers, top programmers, international stars and Premier League footballers. Anyone who performs his or her task pleasantly, co-operatively, efficiently, thoughtfully and loyally deserves more than just a regular salary cheque and a few brief words of thanks as one among dozens or even hundreds at the Christmas get-together.

Whatever our own position in the office, we should be ready to thank:

1. Anyone who takes a phone call on our behalf.
2. Whoever cleans up our rubbish.
3. Those who take the trouble to show concern when they know something is wrong.
4. People from whom we've borrowed things (especially if it was without their permission).
5. Those who've shown patience and tolerance when we didn't.
6. Anyone who stayed behind to help deal with an extra workload.
7. The person who remembered something important that we'd forgotten.
8. The person who never minds going to fetch something we want.
9. Anyone who gives us a piece of much needed advice (yes, even if it's someone we don't like or a superior or both).
10. Security officers, doormen, commissionaires and Jobsworths.

Establishing codes of conduct of this nature and helping to implement them should be the responsibility of someone on the office staff. If no one has been appointed to do this (or even if someone has), whether an office is a pleasant or disagreeable place to work depends on everyone in it. In that way, it is a true democracy.

CHECKLIST

1. Respect the property, opinions and space of others.
2. Wherever possible, foster the team spirit.
3. Biting the tongue may be painful, but it often saves the day.
4. Bad leaders make bad teams.
5. Everyone on a team is entitled to a hearing.
6. Communication should run from junior to senior as well as from senior to junior.
7. Carrots work better than sticks. Praise seldom leads to apathy.
8. If we thank someone who has helped us in a task, they may well help us again.
9. It is not a good idea to hold up one member of an office as a paragon of virtue if we also give the impression that we regard the rest of the office as idle layabouts.
10. Requests for help should be made as early as possible, not as late as possible.

CHAPTER 6

Everyday Office Practice and Etiquette

Who take their manners from the Ape,
Their habits from the Bear,
Indulge in loud unseemly jape,
And never brush their hair.

HILAIRE BELLOC
– *The Bad Child's Book of Beasts*

Each day in an office is made up of hundreds and hundreds of working and social interactions. We bump into each other as we speed to the fax machine, the photocopier, the coffee machine, another desk, another room. We give and accept excuses, we listen to minor tales of woe and solid motorway traffic, we praise and we criticise. We pass comment on how others look, dress, perform. We flirt and we fume, we share jokes and gossip. The ant world – which merely crawls all over itself – has nothing on us.

Thousands of years ago, when we were clubbing small reptiles to death or being torn in two by big reptiles, such niceties and complexities of behaviour were unknown. Life has become ever more complicated and human beings have had to learn how to get on with each other without resorting to the club or the gun. Codes of manners now cover these hundreds and hundreds of daily working and social interactions. We ignore these codes at our peril.

Working dress
We British are a conservative people. We change our style of dress about as often as we win the Association Football World

Cup. Once that is accepted and understood, the rules that regulate what to wear and when are largely a matter of common sense. If the expectation within the office is that men should wear shirts and ties and suits, and that is what every man is wearing, then we would be foolish not to do the same. We may have the most wonderful taste in clothes and it may be a tragedy that we are not allowed to reveal the colourful and stylish content of our wardrobe – but bucking the system usually ends in tears. The bold may ask (politely) why the men are expected to wear suits, and the probable answer will be one of the following:

> because we've always done so, or
>
> because the Chief Executive prefers it so, or
>
> because we are a uniformed team rather than a ragbag of individuals, or
>
> because all our competitors do, or
>
> because we deal with members of the public and this is the image we wish to project to them, or
>
> 'if you're not really happy here, perhaps you should think of moving on . . .'

This doesn't mean that there is no room for any trace of individuality in male office dress. The last thirty years have seen the introduction of a few permissible changes. 'Jacket' can mean a leather jacket, or a casual jacket, or a jacket made of a different material from the ancient worsted. 'Tie' can mean something a great deal more extravagant than it did in the 1950s. Trainers, joggers and converse boots are still not considered suitable accompaniments to a suit – and rightly so, they look awful together. 'Jacket and jeans' looks pretty hideous, but has become more acceptable to the world of fashion and the world of business – but not in the City and not in the boardroom. Any man dressing for promotion would do well to stick to a suit, dark shoes, and a shirt and tie that are on the dull side of startling. Before attempting to set the office by sartorial storm, it's worth checking what everyone else wears. Better to stand out from the crowd because we're exceptionally good at our work than because we have the appearance of a popinjay.

Much of the above also applies to women, though life is a touch more complicated for them. Men are seldom expected to look attractive: women nearly always are. It seems to be more and more accepted that women in business wear suits, though they are permitted a greater variety of materials and colours, and considerably more stylish cuts, than their male colleagues. The most vexing question for women is whether or not they may wear trousers. Few bosses or employers take exception to a trouser suit. Some still do to trousers and a sweater. A woman would be very unlikely to find an employer who ruled against women wearing skirts. However, both male and female employers still believe they can deduce morals, ability, honesty and loyalty from the length of a skirt. It is still sadly true that totally different deductions are made from how men dress and how women dress. Here are a few unfair examples:

1. A man who dresses grubbily, carelessly or drably is a poor soul who needs looking after.
2. A woman who dresses grubbily is a slut.
3. A woman who dresses carelessly or drably is letting her whole gender down.
4. A man who dresses over-smartly is ambitious or gay.
5. A woman who dresses over-smartly is on the make, professionally or sexually, or both.
6. A man whose clothes are old and worn is charmingly eccentric or too eaten up with his work to realise.
7. A woman whose clothes are old and worn isn't giving enough thought to her wardrobe, or is a secret drinker, or is about to crack up, or is poor.
8. A man may be expected to buy and wear unsuitable clothes.
9. A woman should never buy or wear unsuitable clothes.
10. A man advertises his tailor: a woman advertises herself.

There are signs that, slowly and hesitatingly, some of the worst of these disparities are going, but, although both men and women ignore rules of dress at their peril, women who do so are still in far more danger than men (more on this in Chapter 18). In some offices (usually small ones) there are no strict rules, and people wear whatever they like. This is particularly so for those people who work in the 'media', a wonderfully elastic word that covers television, radio, the arts, advertising, music, magazine publishing and lots more. Care needs to be taken even here, however. There are days when suits need to be worn in the advertising office, and too much promotion within a television company almost invariably means 'goodbye' to the comfy woollies and dirty denims.

Displaying other loyalties

Some people like to display their membership of other clubs, societies, old school associations, or, indeed, their political affiliations, by wearing special ties, badges, lapel pins or baseball caps. We feel very strongly about a cause or a religion, a campaign or an issue. In this sad and unfair world in which we live and work there are certain pitfalls that have to be avoided here. Few bosses or office managers take exception to a small cross (denoting adherence to the Christian faith), or the badge of the Boy Scouts Association, or an old school tie (though it's safer to wear such a tie on occasions when it *should* be worn rather than parade one's grand past on a daily basis). Other insignia are less well received. Many offices take offence at badges that show membership of the Anti-Apartheid Movement, CND, Animal Rights groups, and other organisations that they perceive (rightly or wrongly) as posing a threat to the established order. The best thing to do is look around and see what is being worn and by whom. If the cause means more to us than the job, then there's no problem – we can wear the badge and run the risk, which may not be very great anyway.

If, on the other hand, we turn up in combat fatigues sooty with anarchist rhetoric, then we shouldn't be surprised if we are given the well-tailored cold shoulder.

Baubles, bangles, belts and beads

What the fashion industry refers to as 'accessories' is another area of dress which shows a disparity between what women may wear and what men may wear. There's probably nothing in company regulations that forbids a man carrying a handbag, wearing make-up or be-jewelling his fingers, but such ostentation will be regarded as misplaced and will cause embarrassment if not censure. It isn't now considered a crime or a mortal sin for a man to wear an earring, but women still have special privileges here. Some offices do run an almost military regime, with regulations about the style and length of hair (for men and women), and the length of fingernails. Often these regulations come (justifiably or not) under the heading of Health and Safety. It is highly unlikely that anyone would work in such an office without being aware of these regulations, but, if we like to dress extravagantly and hanker for the days of Woodstock and Flower Power, it's something we should consider.

The simplest way to discover what we should and shouldn't wear to work is to keep our eyes open when we visit our new workplace and attend the interview.

Dressing for an interview

This subject has been covered already in Chapter 2, but it's perhaps worth making one small point here. If we are totally confused as to what we should wear for an interview (it's nearly always our suit or our best working outfit – not dinner jacket or ballgown), then we should ask around. Many of the problems to do with business etiquette can be solved by asking the right person what to do *in advance*. If the interview is to be an extended one, and will involve practical tests and assault courses as well as the customary verbal exchanges, then we should have been informed of this and told what special protective clothing to bring.

In our soggy climate, an umbrella is often a very useful thing to take when setting out for an interview. In the euphoria of getting the job, or the gloom of failing, we have to remember not to leave it behind.

Punctuality

Whether we believe that punctuality is 'the politeness of kings' (Louis XVIII of France) or 'the virtue of the bored' (Evelyn Waugh), every employer rates it very highly. It doesn't matter why they do (in Freudian or other terms). It has to be accepted as a fact of life that in the world of business, punctuality matters enormously. To be late for an interview, a meeting, a conference, a business lunch or plain old work, without having a good reason *which has been communicated to boss, panel, client, colleague, customer or whomever at the earliest possible moment* is a grave fault and universally considered to be bad manners. Being late is not a sign of importance or great industry. It's a sign of poor organisation, or thoughtlessness, or rudeness, or stupidity.

All instances of unpunctuality call for an apology, but different circumstances call for different action to accompany that apology.

Run-of-the-mill lateness for work should be accompanied by apologies to colleagues as well as an immediate superior. They may have had to cover for us. They may have had extra work thrust upon them that we should have been doing. They may have had to work in an atmosphere soured by our failing to turn up on time. The apology should be accompanied by a very brief explanation of why we were late – points failure at Kentish Town, child not well, cat dancing on only clean shirt or blouse, etc. etc. No matter how angry we are at what made us late, no matter how thrilling or unusual a story we have to tell, no matter how much we need large doses of sympathy – all that has to wait and take third place. The apology is what matters. And in second place should be some demonstration of concern for our colleagues – have they had to cover for us, etc.?

A friend once told me of a colleague who was almost

invariably late for work, meetings, conferences. He would arrive, dishevelled, plonk his bag on the desk or table (bringing all proceedings to an abrupt halt) and say: 'Don't ask! Don't ask!' This command would be accompanied by dismissive gestures of the hands towards all and sundry. But he worked as a freelance . . .

If we are late for an appointment then the priority above all others is to get a message through to the venue of the appointment to let people there know that we are going to be late. If possible we should speak to the person to whom this most matters (unless he or she is busy) and we should try to give a reasonable estimate of just how late we are going to be. The message should be given clearly and politely (without going into irrelevant details of the terrible time we are having on the M25), and it's always wise to make a note of the name of the person to whom this message is given. If we are going to be very late, then we have to consider whether or not to offer cancelling or postponing the appointment. Some companies have a kind of unwritten (and unvoiced) understanding that forty-five minutes is the maximum time to wait for someone who is late and hasn't made contact. The prevalence of mobile phones in the business world has made failure to communicate probable lateness for an appointment even more inexcusable than it used to be.

Knowing that we are not going to be at the office in time to greet a visitor is more complicated. We still have to get a message through as quickly as possible, but we have also to brief someone to act on our behalf. There are some people so well organised that they are prepared for every eventuality and will have already made special arrangements – most of us aren't like that, and there's something rather gloomy and depressing about those who always expect things to go wrong. Once we know that we are going to be late to welcome a visitor, we have to:

1. Inform the office of this fact and arrange for someone to stand in for us, with the suggestion that it would be

good to make some conciliatory arrangements (coffee, tea or other refreshments) for the visitor.

2. If possible, contact the visitor, apologise, explain what is happening and who will greet them, and give as accurate a forecast as we can as to when we will arrive, offering them the opportunity to postpone or cancel the appointment if they so wish.

It is not good manners to ask someone to lie on our behalf, or pass on an inadequate excuse, or have to invent some wild and unlikely story. It isn't fair to say to any secretary, PA or other colleague 'Oh, just tell them my Great Aunt died' or 'Oh, I'm sure you can think of something to tell them . . .' Many people find telling lies a distressing and unworthy occupation, and, simply to be sordidly practical, many people are very bad at lying and inventing. If we think a lie is the only way out, then we should tell it ourselves, so that we can accept full and sole responsibility if our deceit comes to light.

Warnings and notices
Lateness usually arises unexpectedly, but there can be days when we know in advance that we are going to be late. We may have to visit a child's school, keep a hospital appointment, take the car to a garage for some first aid. Because we know in advance, we are not so much *telling* people that we are going to be late as asking if we *may* be late. There is a world of difference between the two. Permission has to be sought from a superior, but, if we have any choice as to when we take this time off, it's only polite to check first with colleagues as to when this change will create the least difficulties. As much notice as possible should be given of the change. Departing the night before with a casual 'Oh, by the way, I shan't be in tomorrow morning' leads to bad feeling. Far better to approach the subject along the lines of 'I haven't yet checked this with Henderson (the immediate superior), but it would help me enormously if I could come in a couple of hours late next Thursday morning. Is that all right with you . . .?' If

our colleagues ask why, we can tell them. If we don't want to tell them all we have to do is explain that we don't wish to give the reason. Our superiors may insist that we do. If so, we have to explain, but we may do so in confidence.

Under certain circumstances (new-found parenthood, illness in the family, moving house, unexpected changes in travelling routine), people may need to make radical and prolonged changes to their working hours. Communication is important here. The onus is on the person requesting the changes to consult with his or her employers at the earliest possible opportunity, giving details of what changes are requested, why, and for how long. Unless it's commercially impossible for the employers to agree, they should do all they can to accommodate these requests.

Smoothing the way

What everyone should be trying to do in all the above is to make the way as smooth as possible – minimising difficulties, avoiding embarrassment, pre-empting problems, forestalling anger. Indeed, this is the key to almost all office life, the cornerstone of business etiquette. This is what should lie at the heart of everyday office practice. Anyone who gets a kick out of provoking arguments, rubbing people up the wrong way, setting one person against another or generally being unpleasant (and there are such people!) shouldn't be allowed anywhere near an office. Some suggestions as to what to do with persistent troublemakers are to be found in Chapter 11, but, for the moment, let us confine ourselves to the problem of

Dealing with latecomers

Two categories of staff have to deal with persistent latecomers:

1. Superiors, and
2. Everyone else.

On the whole, superiors have the easier task.

Something that it isn't always easy to remember in the world of business is that even troublemakers and mavericks are entitled to civility. The persistent latecomer in an office is a source of much bitterness, but a soft answer may turn away sloth as well as wrath. Here are a few suggestions for the superior/employer:

1. Discover why the offender is persistently late – this may need both patience and persistence.
2. If the offender has a good reason, treat the matter with concern – the aim is first and foremost to solve the problem, not punish the offender.
3. If the offender hasn't a good reason, firmly but politely outline why the lateness is unacceptable.
4. If the offender shows no signs of remorse, or, worse, of changing his or her ways, commence whatever progression of sanctions obtain within the office (more on the Progression of Sanctions in Chapter 11).
5. If the first of these sanctions is a warning, make sure that it is clear and understood.
6. If the offender continues to be late, put the first warning into effect.
7. If the offender still continues to be late, proceed to the second sanction.
8. Etc.
9. Etc., etc.
10. If necessary, dismiss the offender – as W.C. Fields said: 'If at first you don't succeed, try, try, try again, and then give up. No point in making a damn fool of yourself.'

The role of colleagues in this sorry saga is a little different. Having no powers of discipline and control, all colleagues can do is exhort latecomers to mend their ways, and explain how everyone in the office is adversely affected. This, again, should be done politely. With luck, there may be someone in the office who is particularly good at this sort of diplomacy.

Whether the occasion calls for the diplomat to have a quiet word with the offender, or whether it's a case of everyone pitching in with their own contribution, will depend on the nature and attitude of the offender and all concerned. There's no point in trying to bring group pressure if the group all have different views, or if they appear to have the makings of a lynch mob. Whichever approach is favoured, it should be seen as an attempt to solve a problem, not break the spirit of a hardened criminal.

Excuses and how to make them

One of the few things that all of us learn at school is that there is a right way and a wrong way to make an excuse or tender an apology. Unless we are totally divorced from what is going on around us, we learn by observation or bitter experience that to be successful, an excuse must:

1. Have some basis in truth (the more, the better).
2. Be used with discretion, i.e. not too often (the less, the better).
3. Be presented with due solemnity, and
4. Sound plausible.

It must not:

1. Be a tissue of obvious lies.
2. Be presented as though it were a boast rather than an excuse (this is no time for arrogance).
3. Be accompanied by misplaced attempts at humour.
4. Be yesterday's excuse or last week's excuse, served up in a barely disguised new format.

All very childish perhaps, but then making excuses is a somewhat childish occupation. Indeed, many people feel that, as adults, they shouldn't be called upon to have to make excuses. Well, the obvious retort to that is that if they behaved like adults they wouldn't have to, but, if this is the level of argument to which we have sunk, then we are all back in the playground.

Making an excuse is something that we all have to do at some time or another, and the best thing we can do is make the excuse with as good a grace as possible. If we are not able to get to work simply because we are suffering from a monumental hangover, there's no need to enter the world of the Chinese *Fanshen* and publicly denounce ourselves and all our faults. We don't have to specify that we have a hangover. But we do have to say that we are not well. If colleagues draw the correct inference, then so be it – maybe we have long been supplying them with the sort of evidence that points in this direction. We can't lie, of course. If the boss saw us in our alcoholic haze the night before, then it's a fair cop. We have to make our excuse, own up if the accusation is accurate, and take whatever is coming to us. Getting so plastered that we are unable to do a proper day's work the next day is a culpable offence and it's unfair to both our superiors and our colleagues.

If, however, we have a reasonable and justifiable excuse, then we are on happier ground. All we have to do is make the excuse simply and honestly and directly – no need to make a drama series out of it, for, amazingly enough, our misfortunes are of far less interest to the world at large than we imagine. We should spare superiors the gory details, and keep it short, never forgetting the words of Aldous Huxley that 'several excuses are always less convincing than one.'

Excuses and how to accept or reject them
Public executions happily no longer exist. Public shame and degradation is also officially a thing of the past – Captain Dreyfus would be smuggled out of the goods entrance today, rather than marched round the parade ground. Similarly, any kind of rebuke within a company should be given in private. It follows, therefore, that the exchange that might lead up to that rebuke should also take place in private. The latecomer or the leadswinger should be invited into the superior's office

to discuss whatever it is that has gone wrong. It may well be that he or she has a valid reason for their misdemeanour, but that they do not wish their colleagues to hear what it is. And, on the other hand, if they haven't got a good reason, any criticisms or warnings should be for their ears alone. Disciplinary proceedings should never take place in the sight or hearing of other members of staff, no matter how unpopular the offender or how tempted the company is to make an example of him or her.

A reasonable excuse should be accepted, without rancour or resentment, though it is fair enough to point out any complications that have arisen for the company as a result of the aberrant behaviour. This may be necessary because it has had an effect on other staff that needs explanation and appreciation. If the excuse is made repeatedly (if someone is unable to keep to normal office hours because of, say, sickness in the family) then there may well come a time when, although the excuse is accepted, a dialogue has to be opened up as to how much longer these difficulties will continue. Discussions may centre around the possibility of establishing alternative hours, of passing responsibility for some work to another person (temporarily or permanently), of granting paid or unpaid leave for a fixed period, of seeing if there are any other ways in which the problem can be solved or ameliorated. At all times, the superior should avoid giving the impression that having to do this is a dreadful nuisance, a bore, the last straw, ulcer-provoking, etc.

If the excuse is not a reasonable one then it has to be rejected. The manner of this rejection will probably depend on just how unreasonable the excuse is and the attitude and track record of the offender. All exchanges should still take place in private, and in an atmosphere of unprejudiced calm. This is where having a clear company policy on discipline (preferably one that has been communicated to the work force) helps. For more on this subject and more serious problems in general, see Chapter 11.

It should be remembered, however, that some people make

unreasonable or lame excuses simply because they are afraid to reveal the real reason why they are late or have been absent or have been giving their colleagues a bad time. This can be especially true when private or family life is going sadly awry. By and large we can only deal with the facts as they are presented to us, and it is not the role of personnel or office managers to administer psychotherapy, family counselling or faith healing. Nevertheless, if someone who is in all other ways a valued member of a company starts to behave with unaccustomed irresponsibility and offers unlikely excuses, the company needs to reject only the excuses, not the person making them. No company ever gained prestige through rudeness or insensitivity towards clients, customers or employees, which brings us to the subject of attitudes and approaches.

How to address senior staff
As well as knowing the status of everyone in the office, it's also important to know the correct way to address everybody – especially superiors. It's possible to pick up a great many clues from other people – if everyone else is addressing the boss as 'Fats' then maybe we can, too. But it would be unwise to rely on this approach. Everyone else may have been in the office for years, and may have had to earn the right to call the boss 'Fats'. It doesn't do for new pupils to assume that they have the same privileges as everyone else. And there's always the risk that some joker in the office will deliberately mislead us: 'Don't call her Ms Stafford . . . she can't stand formality . . . call her "Jo" . . . we all do.' So we call her 'Jo', and watch her visibly take exception to such presumption, and turn round to see the office joker spluttering into a Kleenex.

The general rule is that it's always safest to err on the side of the over-formal. Unless we have been told to the contrary, we should address any senior colleague as Mr Jones, Ms O'Day, Mrs Powell (the 'Ms/Mrs' dilemma is something that we all need help on, and it should be graciously given by the person concerned). It's a fairly safe generalisation to say that the higher a person is within a company, the less likely they are to welcome being called by their first names or by any nickname. It is best to wait for an invitation to do so from the person concerned before presuming to address a senior by his or her first name.

But there are always many, many exceptions to this general rule. There are fewer and fewer institutions where the old regimes of strict propriety still exist, where not a single first name is known, let alone ever uttered. Many offices operate very happily nowadays on a 'first name only' basis, though visitors may find it a little strange (in the sense of unfamiliar) to hear the lift operator greeting the Chief Executive with a merry 'Morning, Sam.'

A more complicated situation may arise in an office where seniors adopt a two-level or situation specific approach. This is where they are happy to be called by their first names in the privacy of their own office (Les or Ray or Ruth or Lena), but wish still to be addressed as Mr Brown or Mr Anthony or Ms Etting or Ms Horne when in front of other members of staff. Such wishes have to be remembered and respected, no matter how complicated they make life. The wise and canny employee is always sensitive to the abrupt changes of mood and attitude that prevail. It is possible to adopt a very different approach to an employer when we're all together in the pub after work on a Friday or celebrating some great company success. What matters is that these changes never go too far. The borderline between familiarity and over-familiarity is very, very finely drawn, and we cross it at our peril.

Life is further complicated in the office if there are members of staff with titles. The correct form of address of Doctors (of Philosophy) is 'Doctor', followed by the family, not the first, name. Knights should be addressed as 'Sir', followed by the first, not the family, name – 'Sir Ernest'. Similarly, the wife of a knight is addressed as 'Lady', followed by her own first name. After that, whether we start to hobnob with the aristocracy, the Church, the Diplomatic Corps or Royalty, the whole issue becomes such a minefield that it is best to consult a specialist book, such as *Debrett's Correct Form*, that will give us advice on standard forms of address for everyone.

An important lesson to be learnt in any office is how to obtain access to senior members of staff. It's usually bad manners to assume that anyone has time to deal with our problems or queries or complaints or requests at any hour of the day. It's bad manners and professionally unsound to assume that our boss has. It is, therefore, wrong to buttonhole him or her as they dash past, demanding that they give us their full attention on a matter that they know nothing about. If we are dealing with a matter of urgency, then it's permissible to say that we need to see them and to ask politely how quickly that could be arranged. There's a world of difference between a senior saying 'Right now' in answer to that question, and our demanding 'Right now'. Unless we are dealing with a real emergency, then we need to go through the proper channels and make an appointment to see the boss. This will almost certainly mean seeing his or her secretary or personal assistant. It may even be more complicated a procedure than that. Some companies have elaborate machinery for dealing with inter-and cross-departmental requests, and that machinery has to be used. If we don't know how to set about making an appointment with the boss (or, indeed, if this is the right thing to do), then we should ask.

Attitudes to peers and colleagues

A workplace is rather like a family home. Most of the inhabitants didn't choose those fellow inhabitants with whom they have to spend most of the working day. The general ambiance shouldn't be as tense or acrimonious as it is in most families, however, unless employees make the mistake of placing their employers and supervisors *in loco parentis*. A second common mistake is assuming that because some action doesn't bother us, it won't annoy others – leaving caps off pens, leaving untidy piles of papers on a desk, not putting things back in drawers, etc. Colleagues can easily become upset by this sort of behaviour, not so much because leaving the top off someone else's pen is a grave crime, but because the lack of consideration shown towards them is interpreted as evidence that we don't value them, and this can cause much ill feeling. The important thing in office life is that we all somehow rub along together, get the job done, and don't grow to hate each other. To achieve this, we have to curb many of our natural instincts and adopt restrained and abirritant patterns of behaviour.

1. Treat no one as an enemy (this does not mean treating everyone as a friend).
2. Adopt an attitude of well-mannered amicability towards everyone (this does not mean making overtures of friendship).
3. Unless and until we learn to the contrary, we should suppose that everyone is honest, means well, and is doing his or her best.
4. If a colleague asks us for help, we should either give it, or explain why this is not possible.

(Many people find that one of the most difficult and embarrassing situations arises when we are asked by a colleague to lie on their behalf – 'Tell him/her I shan't be in. Say I rang you and that I've had to go to the hospital . . .' Sometimes the request doesn't even come with a ready-made excuse – '. . . I'm sure you can think of something to say . . .' Always there is a stated or implied suggestion that we should acquiesce because of 'friendship', because 'we go back a long way', because 'I'll do the same for you sometime . . .' Whether we do co-operate or not is, of course, a personal decision, but there are good reasons for taking the high – probably unpopular – moral ground. Once we start doing this sort of favour, the requests to continue will almost certainly increase. Far from feeling that we are owed a favour, we are more likely to feel that we have become co-conspirator in a tacky scheme. And, bottom line, there is always the risk that the deceit will be discovered.)

5. If we like one of our colleagues, we shouldn't assume that this is reciprocated, and should wait before leaping into over-hearty overtures.

6. It is a big mistake, bidden or unbidden, to take on the role of messenger between senior staff and colleagues *where the message is personal or conveys bad news* (e.g. dismissal).

7. However great the temptation, we should avoid starting or joining coteries whose main purpose is to create dissension within the office.

8. Whatever our inner thoughts, feelings, and ambitions, we should give the impression that we are treating colleagues as colleagues, and not rivals.

9. If colleagues are promoted ahead of us, we should appear to be happy for them. Similarly, we should be duly modest when success comes our way.

10. We have to find a way of dealing with office collections (for birthday presents, retirement presents, wedding presents, etc.)

If we are happy to make a contribution, then this isn't a problem, but there are occasions when we don't want to, or possibly can't afford to. Anyone who is a temporary member of the office staff or has only recently arrived can decline on the basis that they don't know the person for whom the collection is being made – indeed, this point should be made to them by whoever is collecting when the envelope, tin or jar comes round, along the lines of '. . . we thought it wasn't fair to ask you . . .' This lets the newcomer or part-timer off the hook, but also gives them the chance to go against our expectations and contribute if they wish, feeling doubly noble precisely because it wasn't expected of them.

But there are occasions when we do not wish to contribute simply because we don't like the recipient, or think they don't deserve any present, or feel it would be hypocritical to do so. This can be very awkward, because such feelings are bound to run counter to those of the person who has organised the collection and who is standing in front of us with tin and smile at the ready. The bold will say what they feel. The timid may play for time – '. . . I'm afraid I don't have anything with me at the moment . . .' and hope that it is understood that they won't have anything with them tomorrow or the day after and that they will be left alone. A compromise approach is to say something to the effect that '. . . I'd rather make my own arrangements, thank you . . .' People may guess what our true intention is, but it allows the awkward moment to pass without undue embarrassment on anyone's part.

One rule of etiquette that is universally accepted when it comes to office collections is 'He or she who has not contributed to the present should not sign the card.' To do so is a major breach of good manners, as is attending the party to celebrate the leaving/new baby/promotion and accepting the hospitality that others have paid for.

Attitudes to juniors

One of the most revealing aspects of anyone's character and personality is the way they treat their juniors, in age or position. We all have to treat our bosses with some respect or we get sacked. We all want our colleagues to treat us reasonably, so we try to reciprocate. But we have much more of a choice when it comes to attitude towards those who are our juniors, and choice can often be a dangerous luxury in an office. If we are kind, we may think we are being magnanimous but 'they' may think we are being patronising. If we are unkind, we may think we are being justifiably business-like, 'they' may think we are being tyrannical or conceited. This is why codes of etiquette are created – to take personal choice out of the question of behaviour, and to avoid such misconceptions.

Everyone working in an office should be treated with respect, and the two key elements in showing respect for junior employees are knowing how to address them and not telling them to do something that isn't their responsibility.

The former isn't too difficult. Few people nowadays would

dream of calling an office junior 'lad' or 'lass' (let alone 'sweetheart' – more on this subject in Chapter 18). There may, however, be a fine line between deciding which junior members of staff may rightly be addressed by their first names and those to whom less familiarity should be shown. In some cases the decision is based on age. Few sixteen-year-olds would expect to be called 'Mr' or 'Ms', but quite a few sixty-year-olds would. The decision may also be based on the position held in the office. For some reason almost all commissionaires, doormen and -women or security officers are called by their first names – though newcomers to a firm should always check first whether this would be acceptable to the person in question, by introducing themselves to him or her and asking how they would like to be addressed. Failing the existence of some custom or tradition such as this, it's best to err on the side of formality until it is clearly shown that we can drop any 'Mr', 'Mrs' or 'Ms'. The wise and the well-organised do two things:

1. They do their homework when joining a new office team, ask how members of that team prefer to be addressed, and examine office notice boards, in-house magazines and memos to see if there are any clues.
2. When meeting and talking to members of the team, they keep a careful look-out, to see if there are any signs that they are making mistakes in their modes of address and causing embarrassment or resentment.

Of course, the problem exists in its mirror form. There may be times when senior staff are unhappy about the way they are addressed by junior staff. If a new recruit sweeps in full of misplaced egalitarianism and starts calling everyone by their first names (or worse), then it should be someone's job to take the new recruit aside and advise him or her how to address people properly. If no-one has been appointed to do this (or even if they have) then there's no harm in doing it on an individual basis, finding time to talk privately to the new recruit and put him or her wise – '. . . In the office I should much prefer you to call me Mr Oliver (or Ms Holliday or whatever) . . .'

This brings us to a general guideline in pointing out mistakes made by junior employees. All advice and cautions should be sensitively given in private. What we are after is an improvement in practice, not the breaking of someone's spirit. If this approach doesn't work, then we have to try again, and, if that doesn't work, we are then dealing with possible disciplinary action (see Chapter 11).

One presumption that everyone has to guard against in an office is asking or telling another to do something that isn't their responsibility. Sometimes it's understandable that such a mistake is made, sometimes it's forgivable, occasionally it may be in order. Often, however, it is none of these things. Dumping unfair or unnecessary duties on a junior employee is a grave breach of business etiquette. It may seem vaguely amusing when portrayed in a television commercial, where the boss is depicted as scatty and the junior as the personification of patience and self-sacrifice, but it is bad manners, bad organisation and bad news for the company. Sadly, it is quite common in many workplaces, and bosses are responsible for the most occurrences, in dealings with their own secretaries – more on this in Chapter 7.

CHECKLIST

1. We should dress appropriately for the place in which we work.
2. Smart clothes may be beyond us – cleanliness isn't.
3. We should either be punctual or have a wonderful excuse for being late – preferably the former.
4. If we are going to be late, we should let our colleagues know as soon as possible.
5. If we wish to change our hours of work on a particular day, we must give adequate notice of this – and we should ask if this is acceptable, not assume it is.
6. It is a grave breach of etiquette to place part of our work

burden on the shoulders of others – 'I wonder if you'd mind doing the Ambrose Report for me . . . I'm a bit overstretched at the moment . . .'

7. It helps to have an established pattern of treating late-comers, earlygoers, etc.

8. Excuses should be truthful, reasonable, believable, unrepeatable.

9. We should all take the trouble to learn how to address seniors and colleagues.

10. Attitudes, right or wrong, can make offices heavens on earth or hell-holes.

CHAPTER 7

A special relationship – bosses and secretaries

Why not 'Madam Secretary'?
FRANCES PERKINS, first US woman
cabinet minister, when asked
how she should be addressed (1933)

Introduction

Although it's still true to say that most bosses are male and most secretaries are female, every attempt will be made in this chapter to leave sex aside. The suggestions made here (unless clearly intended or stated otherwise) are applicable regardless of the gender of the personnel, i.e. they apply to male boss and male secretary, female boss and female secretary, female boss and male secretary, as well as male boss and female secretary. Problems that may arise where boss or secretary or both wish the working relationship to develop into a more personal and intimate one, are discussed in Chapter 18.

The special relationship

Not only do bosses and secretaries work every day in close proximity to each other (in neighbouring rooms or even sharing an office), they are engaged on the same work. They share every task, even if their roles in each task are different and clearly defined. A boss will have the job of summoning a meeting and deciding what is to be discussed at that meeting. A secretary will have the job of setting up that meeting, helping the boss select a date for it, contacting all those who are to attend, typing out the minutes of the last meeting, circulating such papers and others, noting down any apologies for absence, etc., and will almost certainly have to attend the meeting itself, to take minutes or keep a watching brief. If either one fails in the allotted tasks, then the meeting will be jeopardised.

So, one of the special features of the relationship between boss and secretary is its interdependence. It is a partnership. The longer boss and secretary have worked together, the stronger will be that partnership. Part of its combined stamina derives from knowing each other's strengths and weaknesses. Conversely, one of the dangers of working so closely side by side may be that the day comes when one side (or both) begins to take the other for granted, or when each assumes that the other will handle some aspect of work and neither does anything.

It may also be an unbalanced partnership. The general presupposition is that a secretary exists to facilitate the work of the boss, by checking appointments, ordering transport, sorting correspondence, and performing dozens of other tasks. Few of us see the boss as the facilitator of the secretary's work. This is a shame, because we should be far less likely, as bosses, to abuse the trust and loyalty of secretaries, if we saw at least part of our duty as helping them with their duties. Teamwork, or partnership, does imply a reciprocal arrangement whereby each member of the team helps the other.

Working in close proximity day after day may bring strength to the working relationship (and a good boss and secretary are a formidable team), but it can also place a considerable stress on that relationship. Few bosses can deceive their secretaries, whether on business or private matters. Secretaries tend to know when their bosses are lying, to them or to clients or to wives and partners or to employees, simply because they are so well informed about their bosses. They *know* if the letter was sent, or if the report completed, or if everything is being done to speed the order. How often secretaries are able to deceive their bosses is a trickier question. It isn't difficult for a secretary

70

to get away with a lie in the short term, claiming to have typed up documents or ordered parts, but the truth has a way of emerging in full horror later on.

The keystones of the relationship

If the relationship between a boss and secretary is to thrive, then there has to be mutual respect. Each has to appreciate the other and what the other is doing. This is just one of hundreds of office situations where the keyword is communication. A boss and a secretary need to know on a daily basis when one of them is ill or suffering in any way that may impair their performance. Many would go further and say that it helps if each has at least a little knowledge of the other's general situation in life, though there are plenty of boss/secretary partnerships that do extremely well without such knowledge and prefer it that way. How they come by this knowledge will depend on the tone of the relationship, but without clear indication to the contrary neither should presume that it is all right to ask probing questions.

The tone of the relationship should also make clear just how confidentially any such information would be treated. In general, any personal information divulged by boss to secretary or *vice versa* should be given the utmost respect. Just as it would be very wrong for a secretary to rush to colleagues and tell them all about the boss's incipient alcoholism or forthcoming operation, so no boss should pass on to fellow directors or executives details of the secretary's financial problems or troubles at home. Hollywood may have given us many instances of a secretary breaking this trust (Billy Wilder's *The Apartment* springs to mind), but, perhaps significantly in earlier days, it gave us examples of great loyalty (John Huston's *The Maltese Falcon*). Less popular evidence exists as to how reliable bosses are at keeping their secretaries' trust.

The other keystone of the relationship is a mutual understanding as to what may be fairly expected from each other. This may be more of a problem for bosses than secretaries, since the very hierarchy of the relationship suggests that it is only the boss who makes demands. That many of these demands are considered unreasonable is evidenced by the number of bitterly humorous lists that circulate among office secretaries, with titles such as 'Twenty Things I Wish I Didn't Know About My Boss' – more on this in the next section. The secretary's duty is not so much not to expect too much of the boss, but not to jib at moderate requests made by the boss.

What a boss should guard against
In general, a boss has to guard against falling into one of the following roles: a bore, a slavedriver, a sloth, a cantankerous teacher, a manipulator and a couple of dozen others. To be more specific, here is a list of some of the more heinous breaches of etiquette:

1. Clock watching – checking up on every minute of a secretary's time when the boss happily spends a couple of hours out of the office having lunch, or decides to go home early because it's such a pleasant evening, or takes the day off because the Australians are playing at Lord's.
2. Hogging the stage – assuming that everyone in the office, especially the secretary, has their eyes and ears open for him or her all the time, so that every muttered word will be heard, everyone will tune in whenever he or she speaks.
3. Interrupting – breaking into an existing conversation or telephone call because he or she has just remembered something that seems important.
4. Projecting – making out that someone else (usually the secretary) is responsible for his or her own mistakes (messages not passed on, documents not properly filed, lack of communication generally).
5. Disappearing – drifting out of the office without leaving word as to destination or likely time of return.
6. Ignoring – not showing the least interest in how the

secretary is coping with what may be an abnormal work load.

7. Sneering – holding a secretary's work up to ridicule or pedantically insisting on giving unwanted and unnecessary assistance with, say, spelling or plugging in an electric typewriter.

8. Meddling – making work more difficult than it need be by interfering.

9. Prevaricating – insisting on minor changes to work just for the hell of it, or to display power.

10. Complicating – dumping a huge extra slab of work on a secretary just as it's time to go home.

There are lots more sins of both commission or omission, but this should be sufficient to give an idea of what to avoid.

A boss should also guard against failing to communicate adequately to a secretary what is required. A good secretary will always ask when he or she feels unclear about any given task, but ultimately the onus is on the boss to get the message across. If there has been a failure to communicate, then the boss should not pretend that it's all the secretary's fault. And a boss should find time to give any extra instructions or go over any points more than once, without breaking into tetchy behaviour or making it appear an unwarranted trial of patience.

Lastly, it is bad manners for a boss to expect a secretary to act constantly and totally as a shield and buffer against the outside world. This is a tricky issue, for many secretaries accept this responsibility without complaint much of the time. It's again largely a question of what constitutes a reasonable demand. For a boss to pretend to be out of the office to avoid an awkward telephone call may be acceptable in some instances, but there may well come a time when the secretary is being unfairly placed in the firing line. Refusing to speak to an apoplectic client, and getting someone else to do so, is cowardly. Asking a secretary to shop for a present for a wife or husband is inexcusable.

What a secretary should guard against

There are fewer pitfalls for secretaries, given they that have to carry out their duties faultlessly. It goes without saying that a secretary has to be polite to a boss, friendly without being familiar, a reliable source of information, a keeper of confidences. At all costs a secretary should resist the temptation to have revenge on an erring boss. No matter how great the temptation, it is not acceptable to blow the whistle on a boss's petty indiscretions towards others (unless the secretary is the victim), and a secretary should keep a low profile if urging those others to take action. Films and fiction abound with stories of romantic relationships that spring up between boss and secretary. Some end in marriage and/or happiness: some end in waspish recriminations and tears. There is nearly always trouble when a secretary has an affair with a married boss (more on office affairs and romances in Chapter 8). It is almost impossible to combine love and work and do justice to both, though some manage it without placing an intolerable strain on everyone else around them.

Perhaps what any secretary has most to guard against is taking a boss for granted – in old-fashioned parlance 'taking liberties'. When two people have been working closely together for a long time, it's all too easy for either one to cut corners in work practices, or leap to conclusions about what is required. Maybe a secretary has dealt directly with some minor matters for a period of months, without referring them to the boss, and the boss has so far raised no objection. All of a sudden these minor matters become problematic. The secretary now calls in the boss, who is enraged that they weren't brought to his attention earlier. Partly because it is the way of the world, and partly because the secretary is at fault, the boss will refuse to take any blame for the mess that ensues. The way to avoid such a sorry scenario is to keep communication between boss and secretary flowing at all times, and this is a shared responsibility.

CHECKLIST

1. The relationship between a secretary and a boss is one of interdependence.
2. Just as a good secretary facilitates the work of the boss, so a good boss will facilitate the work of a secretary.
3. There has to be mutual respect between the two.
4. No matter how compelling the temptation, a secretary should respect the boss's trust.
5. A secretary is not a slave.
6. Although a secretary has to work at the boss's pace, it helps if the boss does everything possible to organise this pace to suit the secretary.
7. It is bad manners for a boss to hide behind his secretary.
8. Love and work are unhappy partners.
9. Revenge should not be part of the secretary's armoury.
10. Neither party should take the other for granted.

CHAPTER 8

Private affairs and public knowledge

Life has taught us that love does not consist in gazing at
each other but in looking together in the same direction.
ANTOINE DE SAINT-EXUPERY – *Wind, Sand and Stars*

It is a sad or happy fact of life, depending on how we view
these things, that when people work together day after day,
some of them tend to fall in love (or tend to think they fall in
love). There is little that can be done about this, it has been
going on ever since work was invented. So our main efforts
should be put into how to deal with the problems thus created,
rather than how to stop the inevitable.

It's a complex issue, for emotions are involved – ours as well
as those of the starry-eyed couple. We may feel disgusted,
amused, appalled, or envious. We may be curious or bored.
We may feel suddenly plunged into old age at the sight of the
office Romeo and Juliet lingering over the photocopier. We
may feel that we, too, would like to be whirling around in the
thrills of a romance. Never mind what we feel: it's what we
(and everyone else) think that matters.

But before we examine the perils and pitfalls of office
romances, it's perhaps worth looking at a related issue –
that of office friendships. We're not so much concerned
here with friendships that spring up in the office, as those
that have been already formed before two people start to
work for the same company – especially those where one
friend has been responsible for introducing the other to the
company. How should we behave when we have recruited a
friend into the office?

77

Just good friends

There is nothing inherently wrong or immoral in helping a friend get a job in the office in which we work. It's wrong, of course, to give preference to a friend in the face of other better applicants, and it's wrong to manipulate any interview or recruitment process to enable the friend to get the job unfairly. But if we have a friend who is clearly well suited to a post, then we have every right to tell the friend that the job is coming up and to help him set about getting it. Whether it's a good idea to bring work and friendship together is another matter, but not one that falls within the scope of what is or isn't good business etiquette. Some people work well with friends. They find that, far from interfering with work, the friendship makes working together easier. Others discover, to their horror, that it's impossible to work alongside a friend, that office routine and discipline kills the friendship, or that the friendship continually gets in the way of settling down to work. A little thought goes a long way to help anticipate which category each of us falls into.

More important, as far as other people are concerned, is not what happens to the friendship, but what happens to the office. If we introduce a friend to the office, help him or her get a job alongside us, there is always the grave risk that we give that friend preferential treatment. This is not simply a case of trying to advance our friend's career at the expense of our other colleagues. It's a matter of day to day behaviour. Here are some examples of what constitutes discourteous behaviour in this situation:

1. Sharing private jokes with a friend.
2. Spending much breaktime (and worktime) in recalling what we and our friend have been doing at the weekend or the night before or when we were at school together.
3. Indicating that there exists a private world, with 'special' names for members of the office staff and a 'special' way of looking at what happens in the office.

4. Seeking to bring the friend into conversations or discussions that don't concern him or her.
5. Giving the friend favoured treatment – e.g. being prepared to stay late to help the friend when we have steadfastly refused to help others in the past.
6. Ramming our friend's many wonderful qualities down the throats of others.
7. Forgiving our friend his or her trespasses (lateness, sliding off early, incompetence) when we are unforgiving towards everyone else.
8. Choosing the best or easiest bits of work for a friend.
9. Expecting everyone else to give the friend preferential treatment.
10. Flaunting the friendship in front of everyone else.

As well as all the problems that may crop up while we are working with the friend, there is always the problem of what happens when the friendship starts to go sour. This is why it's so important not to let the friendship interfere with work or with good office practice. If we have kept the friendship under control while at work, then there is every chance that we may still be able to continue working alongside the ex-friend when the personal relationship has ended.

In general, the most important thing to bear in mind when we have a friend in the office is to be sensitive to our other colleagues. No one should ever feel less welcome, less valued, less trusted or less promising a member of a team simply because they do not share a friendship.

When love breaks out
Falling in love or lust creates enough problems at the best of times. When it takes place in an office it can become a nightmare – for the rest of the staff if not for the lovers. People in love tend to do silly things. They forget that there are other people in the world, other important events, other pressing needs. They believe, albeit subconsciously, that they can attend to their duties with a mind that is at best limping along

on 25% of normal concentration. And, above all, they are oblivious of almost everything around them. They do not realise that their lingering glances are a source of endless irritation to one and all. They do not see the queue forming at the coffee machine while they titter and giggle at the silly mistakes they are making (pushing the wrong buttons, inserting the wrong coins), because they are so enjoying being together. They do not know that their fond farewells to each other, as they separate to spend the next two hours some twenty feet apart at separate desks, are causing an epidemic of nausea to sweep the room.

It's impossible to list all the mistakes that lovers make (not even The Bible and the works of Shakespeare can cover all of those), but here are some suggestions that may help to cut out a few:

1. Lovers shouldn't expect everyone else to share in their joy.
2. Work has to come before passion in paid office time.
3. There is always a limit to people's patience, and the limit is usually nearer than lovers imagine.
4. There are no areas set aside for love-making in most offices.
5. A photocopier is a photocopier, not an *amour-prop*.
6. There are few sights or sounds in life more sickening than two people in the same room phoning each other up in the cause of love.
7. Other people are entitled to the basic civilities in life.
8. Behaviour of a loving nature that may pass uncommented upon in bus or tube may receive bad and damaging publicity in an office.
9. Lovers often go hand in hand. Love and promotion seldom do.
10. If the affair comes to an end it may be impossible to go on working together. If the affair doesn't come to an end it may be impossible to go on working together.

No indisputable guidelines can be given as to what behaviour is permissible and what isn't. There are no rules about the degree of intimacy permissible in an office. The onus is on the lovers to make themselves aware of the feelings of others. It may be acceptable to enter the office holding hands, it may not, so better not to risk it. It may be perfectly all right to show with bright-eyed smile that there is mutual joy at seeing each other, but blowing kisses across the room is probably going too far. Broadly speaking, the more the relationship is kept under control, the happier the rest of the office will be.

Even more complications arise when the passion crosses strata within the office hierarchy. When tycoon falls for telephonist, or manager for message boy, then the path of true love has to be trod very carefully indeed. The best thing for the parties involved to do is to keep quiet about the whole thing. A private secret is better than public resentment. Once such an affair becomes notorious, both parties will be subject to immense scrutiny, and any failing in carrying out their job will be roundly condemned. And, should either or both of the parties already be married, then the condemnation will be bitter. It is not the purpose of this book to tell people how to arrange and run a clandestine affair. Suffice it to say 'be very careful': no arriving or leaving together, no long sessions in each other's offices, no holding hands, no languorous gazes, no lunches together, no notes, no calls, no faxes. In office hours, in the vicinity of the office – nothing.

How to deal with office lovers
There is an old story from the days when the publicly puritanical Lord Reith used to run the BBC. One day he went into a conference room at Broadcasting House, to find one of his announcers and one of his senior officials making love on the conference table. He was appalled. He summoned his assistant and demanded that the two lovers be sacked. The assistant spoke movingly on their behalfs, pointing out that the announcer was a nationally famous figure, and that the senior

official was indispensable within the Corporation. Lord Reith reluctantly allowed both to stay, but assuaged his moral outrage at the disgusting incident by having the conference table burnt.

Few people working in business have the kind of despotic power to match that of Lord Reith, especially when it comes to affairs of the heart. We may wish we could rid ourselves of Tristan and Isolde, so that we could get back to discussing the FA Cup in our spare moments, but we're probably stuck with them. It shouldn't hurt to be tolerant if the couple are behaving with some sense of decorum and propriety. If they aren't, then we have to bring this to their attention in a firm but gentle way.

Like any office admonishment, this needs to be done privately and tactfully. It also needs to be done to the offending pair, not just to one of them. It's amazing how often a message gets distorted as it is passed on. A mild and gentle hint to Rhett may be relayed by him to Scarlett as a totally unreasonable rant. Who delivers the rebuke is open to debate. If there is someone with responsibility for office management, then clearly it may be regarded as their job. But there is sometimes a case to be made for an alternative and more informal approach. Many people more readily accept criticism or advice or disapproval if it comes from a group. Where being summoned to an inner sanctum for a formal caution may result in the guilty party or parties feeling somehow heroic, having their faults casually pointed out at their own desks by their peer group during a coffee break may make them focus more finely on whatever it is that they have been doing that has caused offence. At the same time, however, care has to be taken that this process does not degenerate into a rowdy session where an attempt is made to bully the culprit or culprits into submission.

What constitutes unacceptable behaviour
There is no standard scale of behaviour. How public we make our private lives is partly a matter for the law (if we are

extremely uninhibited) but mainly a matter for our individual sense of decency and dignity. How this behaviour is received by those around us will vary from time to time, place to place. A fond embrace as the office empties in the evening (or, better, just after it has emptied) may be perfectly acceptable sometimes, hideously offensive at other times. The sight of a couple holding hands brings a smile to some faces, a sneer or a leer to others. The patting or stroking of bottoms, and fondling in general, is as much courting disaster as it is courting ritual. What the office Frankie and Johnny have to remember is that all their kissing, cuddling, arm-entwining and adolescent horseplay places everyone else in the office in a dilemma. Are the others to pretend that they do not see what is going on? Or are they to make it clear that they do see what is going on? People in an office shouldn't have to spend any part of their working day having to keep their heads down to avoid seeing something that would embarrass them. Nor should they have to make snap moral judgements about whether it is meet to approve or disapprove what is essentially private behaviour. Neither the boring joviality of the drunkard, nor the early flowering lust of the lover has a place in the office.

Where third parties are involved
There is innocent love; there is also, sadly, guilty love. It may be that one or both of the office Abelard and Eloise has a long-term partner elsewhere. If colleagues know of the existence of this partner, then the amorous behaviour in the office is even more inexcusable, for these colleagues are being asked, indirectly, to condone this illicit relationship. And the day may well come when either Abelard or Eloise's partner attends the office party. This places all those who know of the office affair in a very embarrassing and difficult situation, having to chat with the partner as though there is nothing wrong, when all the time we are aware of the deceit that is taking place. It would, however, be bad manners for anyone to choose the occasion of the office party, or indeed

any other company function, to drag such knowledge out into the open and reveal all.

The general rule here is that married members of the office staff should keep their extramarital romances out of the workplace.

How to avoid scandal

If we become romantically involved with a colleague at the office, the simplest way to avoid being involved in any scandal is to leave that romance outside the office; the further away, the better. Car parks are very public places. Only a mad optimist or someone in love believes that nobody notices who is sitting in whose car and at what angle heads are inclined. Here are a few more cautionary reminders to office sweet-hearts:

1. Don't think that public transport is safe – others from the office may use the same route occasionally if not regularly.
2. Part of the attraction of being in love is that we feel so different. Part of the problem of being in love is that we look so different. Get that starry-eyed look off the face before entering the office.
3. Don't suddenly change styles of haircut or dress – both are dead giveaways.
4. Showing an uncharacteristic interest in Chinese Art or the music of Lutoslawski makes people highly suspicious.
5. Office lovers shouldn't give or send cards or flowers to each other on birthdays, unless intending to do the same for everyone else in the office.
6. When alone in a room, office lovers should remember that it is never possible to spring apart in time when someone else comes in.
7. Few smuggled messages or massages go undetected!
8. Office radar is highly effective.
9. One of the commonest early indications of romance is a

deterioration in work standards clear to all.
10. All the world loves a lover except where time and money are involved.

CHECKLIST

1. There is nothing wrong in helping a friend get a job within our own office – all else being at least equal.
2. Office friendships need to be sensitively enjoyed – they can be a bore to others.
3. Friends should not be given preferential treatment in the workplace.
4. Non-friends should not be made to feel second class citizens.
5. Love is wonderful – work is vital.
6. Not all the world loves a lover, and two lovers can be a pain in the neck.
7. Our public behaviour should never be a source of embarrassment to others.
8. It is almost impossible to have a secret office romance.
9. During working hours there is nowhere in the office in which an affair will go undetected.
10. Outside working hours there is nowhere near the office in which an affair will go undetected.

CHAPTER 9

Office communications

A memorandum is written not to inform the reader, but
to protect the writer.
>   DEAN ACHESON – *Wall Street Journal 1977*

Introduction

The mere word 'communication' strikes terror into the hearts
of all of us. It's the most over-used and misused and abused
word in commercial life. The *crime de la crime* in business life
is 'failure to communicate' – not to send a letter or an order,
not to have invited an important client to a meeting, not to
have acknowledged a memo, not to have faxed New York, not
to have re-ordered stationery, not to have notified the sales
team that the new range of products wouldn't be available
until after Christmas . . . The list goes on and on, with an
entry for almost every day of the year and every member of
staff.

The secret of good communication is careful thought and
planning and the establishment of good habits. Before we
can communicate with others, we have to be able to
communicate with ourselves – we have to be able to
remember what has to be communicated, and how, and to
whom. It doesn't matter whether we retain this information
on paper, in a personal organiser or in our minds (though
this last method is highly dangerous). What does matter is
that we regularly review what we are doing and for whom
our work has implications, and, therefore, what we need to
communicate.

And we have to remember that communication is by its
very nature a two-way process. We have to be able to
receive communications as well as send them. It's no good

firing off memos to all and sundry if we're not going to take any notice of replies and responses to those memos. It's no good dispatching vast bundles of manilla envelopes from the office every night if we never really bother to study our incoming mail. It's no good inviting comments if we don't read them.

Purpose
Every communication must have a clear purpose. In a busy working day, none of us has time to deal with unnecessary communications, whether they're phone calls, notes, letters, faxes, or people sitting on the edge of our desk chatting away about aspects of their work which are nothing whatsoever to do with us. If there is no purpose to the memo, then it shouldn't be sent.

If there is a purpose behind the communication, that purpose should be clearly stated. It may not be Booker Prize literature but there's no harm in starting every single memo with a phrase such as 'The purpose of this note is to . . .' Let others sneer. Reviewing the purpose of the note in our minds should at least ensure:

1. That there really is a reason for sending it.
2. That we know what that reason is.
3. That we make the right decision as to whether this communication is for general consumption or for one or two pairs of eyes only (more on this below).

It will also indicate what form this communication should take. In the days of quill pens and carrier pigeons there was little choice. We are blessed with (largely) efficient postal services, private couriers, telephones, fax machines, E mail and such rapid methods of transport that going in person to Shanghai, Sydney or Stuttgart is a viable alternative.

Written or spoken communication

The quotation from Dean Acheson at the top of this chapter reveals a sad truth about written communications. If we write something and send it, we know we have fulfilled our part of the communication process. The rest is up to the recipient of the note. If, however, we rely on a spoken exchange, then we can assume the message was received, unless it's clear that the person we're talking to isn't listening. It should also be possible to get some idea as to how our communication has been received and what response it provokes. This is where speech has the advantage over writing. But each has its place, its value and its pitfalls.

The value of a written communication is its permanency. Once it's on file, we can prove that we sent it. It means we can't deny sending it, but it isn't the role of a book on business etiquette to give advice on how to deny the undeniable. What is essential is that the person to whom the note was sent can't easily deny receiving it – though many try. The drawbacks of a written communication are that what's delivered cannot be disavowed, the words in the note have only themselves to rely on, and there will always be a certain amount of time lost before we get a reply, even if we're dealing with E mail. For the recipient, of course, this isn't necessarily a drawback. In business matters many of us would like time to think before we have to respond.

The value of spoken communication is that it's immediate, it's direct and it allows an instant response. It also allows both sides to gauge how the other is feeling about the exchange, and modify amplification of the original point accordingly. The drawbacks of spoken communication are that either side can deny that the conversation ever took place, or suggest that it covered a totally different subject, or be very selective in recalling what was said. There's also the risk that tempers may become frayed in the heat of the moment and that things are said which are later regretted.

For more about written communication (forms, language, timing, etc.), see Chapter 15. The most important thing to be borne in mind when it comes to spoken communication is that people do not hear well when being shouted out, when their own tempers have been roused, or when the speaker hasn't sufficiently rehearsed what he or she wants to say. The following are also bad mistakes to make when trying to tell somebody something:

1. Getting their name wrong.
2. Getting their title wrong.
3. Choosing a time when the other person is busy dealing with something else.
4. Delivering a private message in public.
5. Basing the communication on an assumption that is itself wrong.
6. Trying to cram too much into one conversation.
7. Talking to the wrong person.
8. Adopting the wrong tone (e.g. 'hectoring' when it should be 'persuasive').
9. Turning a blind eye or deaf ear to the reply.
10. Failing to date any note, memo, letter or fax.

Assumptions about communications
It is always a mistake to make any assumptions about communications. Here are a few points to bear in mind.

1. Never assume that a letter sent or faxed has been received.
2. Don't assume that if it was received it was read.
3. Don't assume it was received by the right person.
4. It's wrong to assume that what we thought we were saying corresponds to what the recipient thought we were saying.
5. Don't assume that all that was needed to be said, was said.
6. Don't assume that what was said or written in confidence will always be treated in confidence.
7. Don't assume that others will understand why it has

been impossible to phone, fax or scribble a note.

8. Don't assume that it's too late to send a message – it may not be.

9. Don't assume that there's plenty of time to send a message – there may not be.

10. Don't assume that any written message is so unimportant that it doesn't need to be checked for accuracy, appropriateness, spelling, etc.

Types of communication

This section is not concerned with questions of when to phone, when to fax, when to send a typed letter, when to send a personal handwritten note. These matters will be covered in Chapters 15 and 16, dealing with Correspondence and Telephone Etiquette respectively. What we are concerned with here is differing contents of messages, however they are communicated.

It is perhaps a sad fact of life that we spend more time on things that go wrong than on those that go right. We put pen to paper to complain more often than we do to praise. To a degree this is understandable: we should be able to take good, or at least adequate, service for granted. But if we communicate only when a colleague or a supplier makes a mistake, and never when they're showing honest, hard-working reliability, then we're in danger of creating a bad atmosphere. Whatever Attila, Genghis Khan and Adolf Hitler believed, fear is not the greatest motivator. If the only memos we send out within the office are packed with rebuke, scorn, dissatisfaction and accusation, then we are abusing the entire system.

The problem is that we know we have to send information. We believe we have to issue warnings and make complaints. We assume that we don't have to pass on praise. We all write, phone, visit in attempts to prevent errors. All too often we don't do anything to show appreciation for hard work, high performance, increased productivity, or whatever. By failing to congratulate colleagues on their success, we are guilty of bad practice and bad manners.

Public notice or private note?

An office is not a frontier town in the Wild West. We do not have to post notices of wrongdoers:

WANTED
FOR FAILING TO DELIVER THE NORWEGIAN CONTRACT!
HARRY ROSS
HEAD OF SALES

Any communications that deal with an individual's shortcomings should be delivered to that individual, for his or her eyes only. If several people have transgressed, then each is still entitled to a private telling off. If an entire office has shown corporate stupidity, then something is very amiss and it won't be put right by sticking a choleric memo on a wall somewhere. The effectiveness of written anger is greatly overestimated.

If all is going well with one person or one department, however, there's no need to keep it a secret. Many companies deliberately display the names of those who have reached or exceeded their targets for the month. Modern thinking is that by publicly praising one, we encourage (or maybe challenge) others. In terms of screwing an extra effort out of employees it may all be sound psychological sense, but we should be wary of overusing this technique. If the same person is acknowledged as flavour of the month from January to December, there is a good chance that others will lose hope or interest. A letter sent thanking someone for a particular piece of good work is unlikely to remain a secret – most people are prepared to divulge the fact that they've received praise. But, whether the good news is passed on publicly or privately, the important thing is that it is passed on.

It is, of course, vital that all those entitled to recognition for a piece of good work get that recognition. It is an error of the worst and most divisive order to communicate thanks and appreciation to A, B and C and to leave out D. If that mistake is made, then it must be rectified as soon as possible, and an appropriate apology made.

Inviting others to communicate

In the bad old days, no one in authority ever invited comments from staff or employees. The bad old days became a little better and Suggestion Boxes were nailed to walls in factories and offices. Few suggestions of a helpful nature were posted into them, and those that were, were largely ignored. Things are different now. As a matter of good sense and courtesy, it should be made clear in any workplace that comments and suggestions are invited from all who work there as to how practices could be improved. If we believe in any kind of office or workplace democracy, then we have to show that we are prepared to listen to the complaints and the proposals of colleagues and employees. Communication has to be a two-way process.

And, once complaints or proposals have been made, we have to show that they are taken seriously. In the bad old days it was widely reckoned that the Suggestion Boxes were emptied once a month (or less) and the contents burnt without even being read. A communication from any member of staff must be acknowledged. If it cannot be dealt with at once, then the member of staff must be informed of this, and given some indication as to when it will be. Clearly the same applies to communications from clients and customers. One of the criteria by which a business is judged, from within and without, is how promptly, politely and efficiently it responds to the initiatives and the communications of others.

The language of communication

Nearly fifty years ago, George Orwell wrote: 'The great enemy of clear language is insincerity. When there is a gap between one's real and one's declared aims, one turns as it were instinctively to long words and exhausted idioms, like a cuttlefish squirting out ink.' Orwell took immense pains with his own writing, always trying to make his meaning clear and easily understood, never wasting words.

It isn't easy. The awful legacy of all other business letters

93

hangs over us as we try to draft the simplest of communications. We slip back into the world of 'Having received yours of 15th inst . . .', and we are lost. Pomposity flows. Sentences become grotesquely complex, twisting and writhing towards a final clause that makes no sense. A simple letter of thanks becomes Uriah Heep's twelve-minute stand-up routine. The reply to a complaint (which we consider unjustified) becomes a declaration of war. A memo about the photocopier reads like the deranged rantings of a mad Luddite.

Language can be a powerful tool or a mess of broken stones. Here are a few points to consider:

1. We should try to write with one voice whatever we want to communicate.
2. That voice should be the voice of reason – at all times.
3. Simple words and phrases are far more effective than complex ones.
4. A letter that is only three lines long is still a valid letter.
5. Short sentences make sense.
6. Emotional language is seldom good business language.
7. 'Formal' doesn't mean 'long-winded'.
8. By page five any letter is beginning to lose its punch. Maybe a meeting is needed instead.
9. Not everyone understands or appreciates jargon.
10. Written language should be kept as close as possible to spoken language.

Other communications

Many companies send Christmas cards to clients and suppliers. Codes of etiquette have little or nothing to say on this subject and on the question of whether or not we have to reciprocate. If it looks as though any such card is only one among thousands sent randomly across the globe, then there is no obligation to respond. It's highly unlikely that a check will be kept of those who do and those who don't. If, however, there exists a spirit of close co-operation between sender and receiver, then it may be worthwhile sending a card in return. If the card comes not so much from company to company as from person to person, then we should certainly reply.

In the case of invitations, there is no doubt. Any business invitation has to be replied to, whether we are accepting the invitation or not. The more formal the invitation, the more formal the response. A handwritten invitation (rare in business circles) merits a handwritten reply. If the invitation is person to person rather than company to company, then a handwritten reply is also appropriate (there aren't many occasions when it isn't). If the invitation gives a telephone number, then that's how we should reply.

If we wish to ask a favour of someone, unless it's a small request, or asked of a close colleague, it is usually fairer to communicate this in writing. Confronting someone face to face puts them on the spot. If they want to decline, but to do so politely and not cause offence, they have no time to produce an excuse that saves the faces of both parties. It is also not good manners to preface any such request with 'I'm sure you won't mind . . .' or any similar phrase. If the person asked says he or she can't help, it is impolite to ask why not, or to sweep aside the apology.

Turning down a request for help should be done as politely as possible. There is no need to go into elaborate explanations. However tempting it may be, it is not politic to rid ourselves of the person making the request by suggesting the names of other people he or she could try, unless we genuinely believe these people may wish and be able to help.

If members of staff are taken ill and need sick leave, it is good practice to send a letter or card to them showing concern and wishing them a quick recovery. The more serious the illness, the more important it is to write to them, but the more tactful the message needs to be. Humour can be much out of place here. If a close relative of a member of staff dies, then a note of condolence is appropriate. Who should send this note is a matter for the individual company, but it should come from a senior member of staff. The bereaved's colleagues will almost certainly make their gestures of sympathy. Choosing the right words isn't easy at such times, but time and trouble should be spent on this, as a personal message, however brief, will be greatly valued.

NOTE: More on customer complaints and how to deal with them in Chapter 11. More on correspondence in general and how to draft letters in Chapter 15.

CHECKLIST

1. The secret of good communication is careful planning and the establishment of regular practices.
2. Every communication should have a clear purpose – otherwise we run the risk of wasting precious time.
3. We should not assume that written communictions will always be read by their recipients.
4. Shouting rarely helps to convey a message.
5. It helps to communicate good news as well as bad.
6. Some thoughts are best communicated privately.
7. Communication should be a two-way process. We should always be prepared to receive the thoughts of others.
8. Communication is best achieved in clear language – the simpler, the better.
9. Requests for extra help from a colleague are best communicated in writing. This avoids putting the colleague 'on the spot'.
10. Out of sight should not be out of mind if a colleague is ill. A card that communicates sympathy and good wishes will be appreciated.

CHAPTER 10

Reports and reviews

They have committed false report; moreover, they have spoken untruths; secondly they are slanders; sixth and lastly, they have belied a lady; thirdly, they have verified unjust things; and to conclude, they are lying knaves.

WILLIAM SHAKESPEARE – *Much Ado About Nothing*

Introduction

In the old days, reports were private, secret, damning records that nobody was allowed to see but which had the power to smash a career for ever. Today, many reports are open affairs, to which the subject of the report must be allowed access. There is still, however, the sneaking suspicion that for every open, encouraging report there is a hidden, private, secret, damning one, just waiting to smash the subject's career for ever.

Reviews

Many companies have adopted a policy of conducting an annual (or perhaps more frequent) review on individual members of staff. The purpose of this is (allegedly) twofold:

1. To make sure the subject's career is structured and that the best possible use is made of his or her talents, and
2. To scare the wits out of the said subject.

The atmosphere in which such reviews are conducted may well depend on the state of the company or department's own health, and the rough estimate that the review panel has of the subject's performance since the last review. Few reviews are truly open enquiries – they are there to affirm the board's suspicions and confirm their hunches. In general, certain guidelines should be available, and both review board and subject should know the structure that is supposed to exist, and should stick to it.

For the subject:

1. We have to be prepared, not for the worst, but to be able to give a reasonable account of our performance. We have to be ready to justify our past or present salary, and our future existence within the company.
2. We have to present ourselves in the best possible light, and that includes dressing appropriately. A sloppy appearance smacks of sloppy performance.
3. We have to be punctual.
4. We have to be sober – the time for celebration or drowning our sorrows comes later.
5. We should know our rights. If there are rules governing the conduct of such reviews, we should be aware of them. This may be especially true of any rights of appeal against the decision of the review board.

The review board should bear in mind:

1. That there has to be scrupulous adherence to the rules governing such reviews.
2. No matter how appalling the subject's performance *is believed to have been throughout the period under review*, he or she must be allowed a fair hearing.
3. The purpose of any review or report should be to raise the level of performance of the person or department in question.
4. Criticisms should always be justifiable – it's not permissible to hurl the odd extra rock out of spite or because it's probably well deserved. Criticism should, of course, also be constructive.

5. Criticisms or condemnations uttered in a civil manner often have a devastating effect (and deny the recipient the chance to brand the board 'a bunch of lunatics' to his or her cronies in the nearest wine bar that evening).

If a review or report leads to subsequent arguments and recriminations, then there should be a set procedure to deal with these. Matters get out of hand when an insufficient framework exists to deal with the emotional backlash that can follow an unflattering report.

The main purpose of any review should be to locate good performance, encourage further effort, increase an individual's feeling of self-motivation, and identify what is going wrong. Once identified, the important thing is then to present whatever is going wrong as a problem to which we are all seeking the solution.

Written reports
It should always be clear what a written report is about, who compiled it, and at whom it is aimed. Care should always be taken to see that everyone who is entitled to a copy of such a report receives one. This is as much a matter of business efficiency as it is of business etiquette. It is a good idea to compile a list of such people against which to check the dispatch of any report.

Like any other communication within office life, reports should be written as though with a desire to communicate rather than obfuscate information. No matter how glossy the cover, how snappy the binding, how impressively thick the document, how wide the spreadsheets, a report stands or falls by the language in which it is written, and that should be as clear as possible. It also helps if it is written in a professional but natural style. It's all too easy to lapse into a kind of reportspeak, which is notorious for sending readers to sleep on the 17.53 from Charing Cross, the 18.16 from Paddington, the 18.05 from Manchester Piccadilly, etc.

Fatal reports

If a report concludes that Harris or Ms Southern is for the chop, then good business etiquette decrees that we should give them this distressful news face to face. They should not learn of it by opening a letter. The temptation to hide behind a curt little note may be enormous, and our interview with them, at which they learn of their dismissal, may be uncomfortable in the extreme, but the professional fate of employees warrants more than a line or two of printout. If we achieve a reputation for mail order sacking, then we almost certainly set up an office atmosphere where every envelope is seen as a potential letter bomb, and the man or woman who takes round the mail is viewed as the Figure of Death.

A final thought

In companies where the entire staff is given an annual review, it has to be remembered that this same staff will all get together and compare notes about their own reviews. If the same criticisms are hurled at everyone, out of an understandable desire to raise all round performance, then that criticism will lose much of its sting. If it seems that every report is the same report, and that only the name at the top has been changed (like some awful mail shot), then praise doesn't seem like real praise, and adverse comment will seem like general bitchiness. The former will lead to resentment; the latter will allow those who have been justifiably criticised to wriggle off the hook, as far as their own consciences are concerned.

CHAPTER 11

What to do when things go wrong

The customer is never wrong.

CESAR RITZ 1850–1918

Two wrongs don't make a right, but they make a good excuse.

THOMAS SZASZ – *The Second Sin*

Introduction

When things go wrong two things usually happen: people make complaints, and somebody gets the blame. This chapter is concerned with both. In any well run business, mechanisms are already in place to deal with mistakes and/or incompetence. These mechanisms, however, are almost certain to have been established with a view to taking whatever steps are necessary to avoid or to limit legal liability. Moral obligations may not have been given the same priority. As far as most businesses are concerned, the main trouble with complaints is that they cost money. Dealing with an unjustified complaint can be expensive enough. Dealing with a justified complaint can break the bank, or the shareholders' hearts. Whenever anyone complains, whether supplier, customer or employee, a company's first concern will always be to cover itself legally, to instigate a damage limitation exercise. There are parallels here with the world of motor accidents. One of the first rules of insurance, drummed into every motorist's subconscious by their insurance company is 'whatever happens, never admit to your own culpability'. It may be a natural reaction and the polite thing to say 'sorry' to someone we've just run over, but we mustn't do it. There are some for whom being in business is as passionate as being in love, and means never having to say (or being allowed to say) you're sorry.

Those who wish to occupy the moral high ground may sneer, but it is one of the hard facts of business life that what is politic comes before what is polite. This doesn't mean that the niceties of etiquette have no place in dealing with complaints, however. Far from it; our chances of weathering any legal storm or emerging victorious from any legal tussle are much increased if we adopt a civil approach to our adversaries. Judges, industrial tribunals, juries, inspectors, bosses, customers and employees alike all tend to put a more sympathetic interpretation on what is said civilly than on what is said rudely. We rant and rage, insult and deride at our peril. So, in our tough world of business, we should all be encouraged by the fact that there are times when what makes legal sense also makes social sense.

The other reason why complainers are so unpopular is that dealing with complaints takes a lot of time. However nit-picking a complaint may be, we have to deal with it. If an irate customer phones with some petty accusation, we have to speak to that customer, take note of what he or she is saying, promise that the matter will be investigated – and then keep that promise.

Internal complaints – those from within the office
It is always a good idea to have a known and established machinery for dealing with in-house complaints (a person to whom the complaint should be made, a committee that sits to hear complaints, an accepted practice of bringing both sides to the complaint together, etc.). This often helps to stop matters getting out of hand for several reasons:

1. It means the matter will be handled by someone with experience in dealing with complaints.
2. It means that any argument as to how the complaint

should be handled (or by whom) will be circumvented.
3. It means wasting as few people's time as possible.
4. It means that both sides in what is, to all intents and purposes, a dispute will have some idea of what to expect.
5. It makes any ultimate decision a less personal matter – i.e. it doesn't look as if management sided with one party against the other from the start.

Whether this machinery exists or not, however, certain basic principles apply in dealing with any complaint:

1. A pleasant manner and an apparently sympathetic approach is always helpful.
2. The sooner an attempt is made to handle a complaint, the better.
3. Approaching the matter as though there is a problem here, and the aim of all concerned is to solve that problem, lessens the risk of a legacy of bitter personal animosity, either between the two sides to the dispute or between the 'loser' and the company itself.
4. Every opportunity should be given to the two sides to find their own acceptable solution to the problem (as long as that solution is compatible with office discipline).
5. People who complain should not automatically be regarded as trouble-makers. There is such a thing as a justified complaint.
6. A complaint should always be dealt with at the most modest level possible – don't bring in the company solicitor to deal with a wrangle over who should park where in the office car park.
7. The imposition of discipline should not be seen as an exercise in power.
8. If two people have been asked to work together and they are incompatible, something has to be done about it.

In the case of an internal complaint in an office, we are really dealing with a three-party issue: the complainant, the person complained of, and the company itself. Each party has obligations. Each party should know how to behave. No one side should seek to turn the complaints procedure into a slanging match or a fight to the death. Most internal complaints within an office fall into one of two categories: performance and attitude. 'Performance' complaints relate to punctuality, not doing the job properly, passing work unfairly on to others, leaving early, spending too long over lunch, losing things, borrowing things, etc. 'Attitude' complaints relate to how a person is treating his or her colleagues – showing too little respect, taking people for granted, being rude, getting people's backs up generally. Problems of sexual harassment are covered in Chapter 18.

Making a formal complaint
A complaint about a colleague should be made to the right person and in the right way. There is a world of difference between seeking some kind of improvement in a colleague's performance or attitude and seeking to turn the rest of the office into a bloodthirsty mob braying for the culprit's dismissal. Unless there are good reasons not to, it is best to let the culprit know that we are going to make a formal complaint, to whom and why. It gives the culprit a chance to make an eleventh hour improvement or at least to offer some kind of apology and make a promise to do better in future. That may be enough to solve the problem. If, however, there is no improvement and the promise turns out to be an empty one, then the culprit cannot say that he or she hasn't had fair warning.

Once we have said that we are going to make the complaint, we should go through with it. Office pests, bores and leadswingers are like children: it's no good saying we are going to take action and then not doing so; that only encourages them to perseverate their naughtiness. Although it's very understandable that we should make a complaint when we are angry, we should try to do so coherently and with all signs that we are patient beyond belief but have been forced to take this reluctant action. Racing off to the boss, screaming and thumping desks isn't the best way to make a point. We then appear hysterical and unreasonable. It also may be a bad time for the boss who won't then give us a sympathetic hearing. Better to bite our tongues in the short term and make an appointment to see the boss (or whoever deals with internal complaints) at a convenient time. We may then prepare our words carefully, making sure that we limit the complaint to whatever really is wrong, and don't go plastering much ill-will and bad temper all over the place.

If the boss (or whichever third party will be hearing the complaint) decides that the complaint should be made in front of the culprit, we should agree to that plan – unless we have very good reasons otherwise and are prepared to explain what those reasons are. It will be up to the third party to make sure the hearing doesn't get out of hand. Again, the important points to remember are to make the complaint reasonably, to avoid getting into a slanging match, to cut out all attempts at character assassination of the culprit, to be specific as to what we are complaining of, and to adopt a generous (or at least reasonable) attitude to any proposed solution to the problem. What we have to remember is that our critical view of the culprit may not be shared by those who are hearing the complaint. After all, they decided that this person, that we abominate, was worth employing in the first place. We may want the culprit thrown on to the street: they may value him or her as an asset to the company.

Obviously, if we know of other colleagues who have been similarly upset or annoyed by the culprit, it is a good idea to ask them if they, too, would like to make a formal complaint. If we're not too sure, we have to take care that we don't appear to be trying to stir up antagonism towards the culprit where none exists. This is a matter for careful thinking and considerable tact. In general, however, a complaint made by several people is treated more seriously than that made by a single individual. In this situation, however, we have to guard against the sudden disappearance of this promised support when the time comes for action. It is no bad thing to make a note of any similar grievances that others express towards the culprit. This makes it much harder for those others to withdraw their support at the last moment.

Giving criticism
It is essential to bear in mind that all criticism, positive or negative, should have only one aim – to improve whatever weakness or fault or bad behaviour is apparent in the person being criticised. Without such an aim, criticism degenerates into a wholly destructive force that will create an unpleasant atmosphere in the office for everyone who works there. This means that criticism should always be specific – just who and what are being criticised must be clear. It's no good telling people that they do everything wrong, that there isn't a single aspect of their work worthy of praise, that they are totally inept. A criticism should highlight one aspect of their work or behaviour. No matter how bad they are, they can improve only one step at a time. Tell someone he or she is worthless and they won't know where to start trying to improve. Tell someone that they take far too long to answer correspondence and at least they'll have a pretty good idea of what they need to do. Tell someone that they should answer letters more promptly and they'll know exactly what they need to do.

However it is voiced, all criticism must be justified. Specific examples of what is going wrong should be cited to whoever's being criticised, to help them focus on what they are doing that is wrong. If they are using the company telephone to make private calls, there must be evidence of this. Without such evidence a flat denial on their part cannot be refuted, and then there is the added problem that they may gladly wear a martyr's crown and tell others in the office that they have been unjustifiably criticised – 'They tried to pin that on me and they couldn't.' Any such evidence should be produced calmly, avoiding the worst excesses of the French Revolution. Difficult though it may be, there should also be no suggestion in the way the criticism is made that a team of secret agents has been watching every move the wrongdoer has made in the office over the last six months.

Only if an office is working with an unnatural amount of efficiency should any criticism be petty (and even then it's not a good idea, since it may well sour an otherwise good atmosphere). There is very little point in moaning about the way some member of staff leaves a desk littered with paper clips if the bailiffs are poised at the door and the firm is about to go bust.

Delegating to others the task of voicing a criticism is acceptable in only a few cases, e.g. where the criticism would be overwhelming if it came from the Managing Director but would sound weighty but not crippling if it came from, say, a Head of Department. In general, if anyone in authority feels there is cause for criticism, then he or she should be the person to voice it. It's always possible to turn to someone in higher authority if the person criticised does nothing to improve matters. Turning to someone in lower authority, however, when the boss is bored, merely looks as though the original criticism was but a half-hearted gesture.

Handing over the task of making the criticism to another always runs the risk of that criticism being poorly expressed, or unfocused, or lacking the weight of personal experience. 'I hear you've been . . .' is a less impressive opening phrase than 'I know you've been . . .'

Finally, it's worth while remembering the words of Somerset Maugham: 'People ask you for criticism, but they only want praise.' We shouldn't be surprised if criticism, however sensitively made, however justified, however needed, is coldly received.

Taking criticism

The immediate and natural and childish reaction to most criticism is to reject it. No, we think to ourselves, we haven't been late, we aren't rude, we do put files back, we don't go out of our way to annoy others, we are pulling our weight. Even if the criticism is totally unjustified, however, and our indignation is rightful to the extreme, we should not lose our tempers. If we wish to set out to prove that we are being wrongly appraised, then we shall need cool heads and calm nerves. It's a mistake to get hot under the collar, for too many people are aware of the quotation from *Hamlet* – 'The lady doth protest too much, methinks' – although they usually get it wrong and attribute it to the wrong character. If we screech and scream to the person confronting us with our alleged fault 'Why don't you ****** ***!' or 'Oh, so I'm lazy, am I? Well, you're an **** ***' we do little to establish ourselves in the eyes of others as the sort of reliable, conscientious member of the team that would never put a foot wrong.

If the criticism is justified, then we have to accept it with as good a grace as possible. None of us likes having our faults listed (the longer the list, the worse we feel), but none of us is perfect so we all do have faults. If the criticism is made in an unfair way, however, or at the wrong time, or in front of the wrong people, then we may rightly point this out. Once a colleague or someone in authority has pointed out what we are doing wrong, then the next step is largely up to us. If we can't remedy the situation without the help of others (there's too much work for any one person to do), then we must ask for that help. If the solution lies entirely in our hands (we need to get up a little earlier to avoid being late every day), then we should acknowledge this and take the necessary steps. If there is no solution to the problem (someone at home is ill and we have to look after them), then we have to explain this situation and ask for understanding and tolerance.

If the criticism is unjustified, then we need to point this out immediately. Again, we have to tell the right person at the right time in the right way, for what we are really doing in not accepting the criticism, is making a criticism ourselves.

Dismissals

Whatever euphemisms may be in current use ('prepared to release you . . .', 'think you'll do better with another firm . . .', 'not taking up the option on your contract . . .', 'allowing you the advantage of early redundancy . . .'), the sack is the sack and all the honeyed words in the world won't change that. It's a sad day for everyone concerned when someone has to be sacked, but that doesn't mean that all pretence at good manners should go by the board.

A person being sacked is entitled to decent treatment. News of dismissal should be communicated by whoever is in responsibility, in private, face to face with the person being sacked. Certain points may be helpful:

1. Sacking someone should be done humanely, in much the same way that a good vet puts down a loved pet.
2. It should be done without any blustering or bitter recriminations.
3. A reason should be given for the dismissal.
4. If whoever is being sacked starts to argue, then the person in authority should try to avoid being drawn into that argument – it will only end in a blazing row.
5. It should appear to be done more in sorrow than in anger.
6. If whoever is sacked starts to cry, they should be given the opportunity to do so, with as little loss of dignity to either side as possible.
7. It is best to keep the interview as short as possible. This is no time to start discussions on redundancy terms or 'how will you manage financially?' Better to allow the person being sacked to swallow the bad news and beat a hasty retreat to the washroom or wherever to scream, cry, smoke, smash something, etc.
8. On the other hand, it may be an appropriate moment to express general support or sympathy, or at least thank the person being sacked for their contribution to

the company's progress (no irony or sarcasm under any circumstances).

9. If the person being sacked expresses a wish that they would prefer news of their dismissal to be kept quiet, that wish should be respected as far as possible.

10. If someone is to be sacked, they should be informed of this as soon as possible.

Only if it is absolutely impossible to face someone to give them the sack should such news be conveyed by note or letter (never by phone and never by fax!). Apart from the fact that it's bad manners to sack someone in this surreptitious way, there's also the danger that the note will go astray or that the person being sacked will deny getting the letter, and that will in turn lead to a far more harrowing personal encounter.

It has increasingly become the practice to sack people and order them to clear their desks and be gone in one and the same day. There are even cases where management have deemed it necessary to have the person sacked escorted from the office premises – shades of the court martial of Alfred Dreyfus, and we all know what that unfortunate event led to. Though it is just possible to imagine situations where this might be justified, it's by and large a sad reflection on the way business morality has declined. In the bad old days people were sacked with scant regard for their feelings or dignity: they were literally thrown out on to the street. Then came a brief period when people were sacked with some regard for their dignity and with some appreciation of their worth. If, today, people receive written notice of their dismissal and are ordered off the premises within a couple of hours, then something has gone very wrong indeed.

Leaving a job, especially unwillingly, can be one of the most traumatic things that can happen to anyone. Depriving that person of the chance to say goodbye to colleagues and workmates is as unkind as it is ill-mannered. Such practices also breed fear in the rest of the workforce, and fear is never a good motivator. I remember visiting an office one lunchtime a couple of years ago. On other visits there had been a warm and friendly atmosphere. On this occasion all was gloom and frigidity and bitterness. The reason was that half a dozen people had been sacked that morning, with no prior notice, and they had been told to leave immediately. A brave soul (not one of the dismissed) had approached management and asked why this had been done so officiously and so precipitously. He had been told that the management had thought others would worry about their own jobs if notice had been given to those dismissed. But now, said the management, the rest of you can go on working knowing that you won't be sacked. It was impossible to explain the illogicality of this view to them. And one of the strongest feelings among those left in the office was anger that they had not had a chance to say goodbye to those who had been sacked. In any well run business, the polite way of doing things will always be the way that avoids the worst repercussions and creates the least ugly scenes.

Given that such crude practices exist, however, the least that the rest of us can do is to help those in distress. If someone has been sacked and ordered to clear their desk immediately, then we may offer to lend a hand. We may actually assist in clearing out desk or filing cabinet, undertake to send on any mail that arrives, help access personal files on computer, race round to the local for a quick last drink together at lunchtime (if this isn't too poignant), organise some speedy collection on the victim's behalf, etc. One way of seeking to bring comfort and reassurance to the person sacked is by promising to tap any contacts we may have elsewhere in the hope of helping them find another job. Even offering to keep a look out in Situations Vacant columns may bring some relief.

It may be, however, that the person sacked doesn't wish the sad news to be broadcast round the office by a sympathetic colleague. In this case these wishes must be respected even if it means indulging in white lies. There are those who understandably prefer their departure to be interpreted in other ways – seeking more qualifications, wanting to broaden their horizons, aiming for promotion elsewhere, or simply feeling it was time for a change. If this is how the person sacked wishes to play it, then there is little harm in abiding by their wishes, at least in the short term. Once they have gone, the time may come for the truth to be told.

In all this, much may depend on the age of the person being sacked. Although it's always upsetting, being 'made redundant' is such a common event these days that it's no disgrace for anyone (unless there is evidence to the contrary), and certainly not the final blow for someone young – though it is a mighty blow to anyone's self-esteem. The nearer we are to retirement age, however, the heavier the blow, with far less hope of re-employment and perhaps dreadful implications as to the eventual size of our pension.

Being sacked

Having just received the dreadful news, our last concern may be how to behave, but there are certain dos and don'ts:

1. Do try to listen to the rest of what is being said or to read the rest of the letter.
2. Do try to control temper – it doesn't help to be made redundant and be arrested for assault both on the same day.
3. If it's confined to verbal expression, however, anger has its place – both to show management what we think of them and to make us feel less impotent.
4. Don't get down on the knees and plead for another chance – it won't make any difference, and dignity, once lost, is hard to recover.
5. Don't seek revenge for dismissal by smashing machines or stealing important software or setting fire to the office block. It won't take a Sherlock Holmes to guess who's responsible.
6. Do try to make plans for the future rather than to brood on the past.

112

7. Justified complaints against the company who sacked us are OK, slander and libel aren't, and won't help our subsequent career.

8. Do try to find time and the mental resources to listen to and to respond to any kind or helpful things that colleagues are saying (remember, poor old Sydney Carton was politeness itself on the way to the scaffold).

9. If the dismissal isn't instant, but a length of notice has to be served, then we should work that notice as professionally as possible.

10. In all the anger and disappointment that may be raging within us, we mustn't overlook our rights and our belongings – we mustn't leave personal property behind, and we mustn't miss out on any severance pay or redundancy money to which we are entitled.

Incoming complaints

Although we may appraise a person's work by how well they perform, by what goes right, we often tend to judge a person's worth by how they respond when things go wrong. A great deal of time is spent in any office dealing with complaints, and anyone who can do this well is worthy of respect as well as a good salary. A wise company will always value the employee who can keep cool in the face of some repetitious old bore who's fabricated a complaint for little or no reason, or, worse, in the face of someone with a real grievance. The response to anyone making a complaint, however trivial the complaint and however lowly the complainant, should always be positive. A negative reaction to a complaint only fuels bad feeling.

Whoever the complaint comes from (be it wealthy and important client or customer, or 'just an ordinary bloke, mate'), the same rules should apply:

1. Do make it seem, from the initial response to the complaint, that there is a desire to help.

2. Don't shunt complaints around, passing them on to

someone else simply because the complainant is a pain in the neck or dealing with the complaint is going to involve a considerable amount of work.

3. Don't deal with complaints that fall within someone else's area of responsibility – such self-sacrifice only leads to confusion and probably more complaints.
4. Don't be afraid to call in higher authority if things are getting tricky.
5. Don't drop colleagues in it by saying (or suggesting) to the complainant that it's always 'their fault'.
6. Don't make promises that can't be kept simply to mollify the complainant.
7. Do take time and trouble to understand just what the complaint consists of – not always easy if the complainant is in a foul temper.
8. Don't make any soothing offers that may be interpreted as attempts at bribery – there's a vast difference between sending a compensatory pair of tickets to the opera *after* things have been sorted out, and sending a pair of tickets to the opera seemingly instead of dealing with the complaint.
9. Do stick rigidly to the established company policy when dealing with complaints.
10. If there is any doubt as to how the complaint should be handled, then someone in authority must be consulted.

Making an informal complaint
If we wish to make an in-house complaint (about someone or something within the office), then we should follow any procedure that exists. Where there is no such ready-made structure, then we have to invent our own. Most in-house complaints concern people rather than procedures – a colleague is habitually rude, sexist, racist, late, idle, unpleasant. There are occasions when personal criticisms have to be made – someone is smoking in No Smoking areas; someone isn't washing enough; someone is dressing with an aggressive lack of conformity; someone is adopting

an extravagantly anti-social attitude. According to the old adverts, it is the duty of the culprit's best friend to point out that their breath or their feet or their armpits are causing nasal distress. But the best friend may not wish to do this, or the culprit may well not have a best friend in the office (or anywhere else, for that matter). The best approach here is the direct and informal approach. We need to take a deep breath (unless the complaint is of an olfactory nature), and explain to our colleague just what it is that he or she is doing that is causing upset. This should be done in the spirit of 'I'm sorry to have to bring this to your attention . . . I'm sure you haven't realised it but . . . I wonder if you would mind . . .' The impression given should be that there is a problem and we are looking and hoping for a solution – not that we are out to cause trouble. That is why it's always best to make the complaint as soon as we are aware of the rudeness, sexism or whatever. If we wait, with increasing impatience, while our colleague indulges in his smutty stories day after day, then when we do finally decide we can't stand it any more there is always the risk that we shall over-react, that we shall rant and rage and scream at the colleague. 'And all I did,' he or she will say later, 'was tell one little joke.' Of course, it wasn't one little joke, it was the last little joke in a line of hundreds, but that isn't how it will seem. If we are going to complain, we should complain early.

There are those who recommend subtle, ironic, or even sarcastic ways of complaining. If we are assailed each morning by someone's over-powering scent or aftershave, the theory goes, we should purposefully open a window or start fanning ourselves briskly with a sheaf of papers. Each to his own, but such methods have several drawbacks:

1. Many offenders are too thick to understand the point that is being made.
2. There is always the risk that the offender thinks we are all having some kind of game.
3. Lots of offices don't have windows that open.

115

4. There's no way we can accuse someone of sexual or racial offence by gestures.
5. We shall almost certainly have to continue to repeat the gesture indefinitely.

If the direct and informal approach on our own doesn't work, then we have to try other methods. Most bores and layabouts don't annoy only one person in the office. If we look around, we may well find allies. There is no harm in carrying out a kind of consumer survey, asking others 'Could you live in the office without Morton's hourly animal noises?' or 'Do you ever wish that Welk would use a handkerchief?' If no one else has yet noticed the offending behaviour, they may well do so once it has been pointed out to them. But it's more likely that there are others as annoyed as we are. The next step is to consult with fellow sufferers as to what should be done. Again, the direct approach is usually the best. When several people gather around Morton's desk or knock on Welk's door even the most hardened villains feel a moment of fear. The more complainants the better, but we have to beware of overdoing the complaint. Morton and Welk must be left in no doubt as to how they are upsetting people. The group mustn't all shout at once, vying with each other as to which is the most important complaint. One fault at a time is sufficient.

(A word of caution – it is not unknown for people to say they will join in group action and then fail to turn up at the appointed time and place. If others have promised to support us in making a complaint it's best not to assume that they will keep that promise. The more serious the complaint, the more this should be kept in mind.)

There are times when the direct and informal complaint doesn't work or is inappropriate. At such times we have to consider what more formal methods are available to us. Here are a few points worth remembering:

1. We should always be sure of our facts.
2. It should be apparent that we are looking for an

improved situation, not a public execution of the offender.

3. We should take our complaint to the right person: it doesn't need the Company Chairperson to deal with someone sloping off twenty minutes early each night.
4. We should examine our own performance in the office – tit-for-tat can be a most unpleasant experience – although the fact that we are not perfect shouldn't stop us making the complaint.
5. We should be prepared for the inevitable question from the person to whom we complain: 'What do you expect/want me to do about it?'

External complaints

A complaint from outside the office, from a customer or client, is a different matter. If we are making the complaint, then the first decision we have to make is whether we are going to complain in person, on the phone, or by letter. Turning up in person has its disadvantages. We may well catch the company on the hop, but this doesn't mean we shall necessarily have our complaint attended to any more swiftly or effectively. Arriving on the doorstep unheralded and uninvited may appear rude, and rudeness doesn't help our case.

Telephoning has its advantages and disadvantages. It certainly can't be considered rude, and an unexpected phone call can elicit a great deal of useful information – the general attitude of the company to complaints, the lack of any established mechanism to deal with complaints, the reluctance of anyone within the company to respond to the phone call, etc. Any complaint made on the phone should be followed up by a letter. A careful note should be made of whom we speak to, their position in the company, and of any action that they have promised to take. It's not a bad idea to record the telephone conversation, in which case it is polite to inform the people to whom we are speaking that this is what we are doing.

Complaining by letter also has its strengths and weaknesses.

There is always the danger that, rightly or wrongly, the company to whom we send the letter of complaint can say they never received it. Recorded delivery can help here. A letter has a permanence to it – once received it shouldn't be ignored. And there's that comforting feeling when we write a letter that we have the stage to ourselves. No one can interrupt and say: 'Ah, but you see, it's never been our company's policy to . . .', or 'May I just stop you there and point out that . . .' On the other hand, no dialogue takes place until we get a reply to our letter, and that reply will be entirely in the hands of the other side. Letters can be exchanged for weeks, months, years and little or no progress made. Sometimes a combination of methods is best – a letter, promising a follow-up phone call, say, a week later. That phone call must then be made.

In all complaints, it is essential to keep a record of what is said, to whom, by whom; what action is promised, when; what we say and what they say. We should never threaten any action that we don't intend to take. We should never be rude, despite provocation, and if the other side is rude, we should point this out and contrast it with our own good manners. We should always ask to whom we are speaking, when on the phone, and note to whom they are referring us. It all takes a great deal of time, but in the long run it's worth it, once we get satisfaction.

Bad news and how to handle it

Apart from notices of dismissal (see earlier this chapter), there are other items of bad news that may have to be relayed within an office. Contracts may be lost, perks whittled down, bonuses cancelled, staff facilities lessened – or there may be some bad news of a personal nature, concerning an employee's family. There is always a great temptation to persuade someone else to pass on bad news, but, if it is our job or if it seems right that we do it, then we have to accept that responsibility. Bad news should be delivered gently, privately and informally. The more serious it is, the more care should be taken in its delivery. If it comes as a shock to the recipient then allowance should be made for any emotional response or bizarre behaviour. Bad news is a time for breaking rules or putting them in abeyance. It is not a time for sticking to protocol.

CHECKLIST

1. There should be an established machinery for dealing with in-house complaints.
2. Complaints, wherever they come from, should be received politely. Resentment should be hidden.
3. Complaints should be made to the right person in the right way.
4. The purpose of criticism is to improve performance and ameliorate the situation.
5. Criticism should not be automatically rejected.
6. Personal criticism should be privately made.
7. A person being sacked is entitled to decent treatment.
8. A person being sacked may respond in an emotional way.
9. Before we complain we should be sure of our facts.
10. Bad news should be communicated in a sensitive way.

CHAPTER 12

Privacy in the office

I might have been a goldfish in a glass bowl for all the privacy I got.

SAKI (H.H. MUNRO) – *The Innocence of Reginald*

Only the family and the armed forces allow less privacy than most offices or workplaces. Managing directors and chief executives are better off than most of us, for they have an inner sanctum to which they may retreat when someone or something is getting on their nerves. Most of us work cheek by jowl with our colleagues, enjoying at second hand the garlic that laced their last night's repast, inhaling their astringent aftershave, listening fascinatedly to their every tummy rumble. Few of us feel in a position to insist that they cease their rambling anecdotes on life when they were young, or the progress of United in the League, or what constitutes 'a good laugh'.

But the line can and must be drawn somewhere, and the issue which has brought the subject of privacy within the office to the fore is that of smoking.

Smoking and other fumes
Whatever the rules within the office (and most offices nowadays are No Smoking areas), there is no excuse for inflicting tobacco smoke on others. There is enough evidence to show that passive smoking can cause lung, throat and stomach cancer to make smoking in the office the most heinous of all offences and the worst possible breach of etiquette. It shouldn't be necessary for anyone to have to ask another to put out a cigarette, but it sometimes is. The request may be made politely, but very firmly, and we

121

shouldn't take 'no' for an answer. If the smoker is obdurate in his or her murderous intent, then we must complain immediately. It doesn't matter how friendly the offender is at all other times. It doesn't matter how charming, helpful or courteous he or she can be. It doesn't matter how little cigarette there is left to smoke. Smoking kills, cripples and incapacitates.

But there are good smokers, just as there are good dog owners, and they should be shown courtesy and consideration. If they need a cigarette, then it's good policy to provide them with a place where they smoke in peace. Increasingly in London and other cities, little knots of smokers are to be seen huddled on the pavement outside their offices, in the coldest of weather, puffing away, stamping their shoes to allow the blood to circulate to their feet and trying desperately to warm their hands by the tiny glow of the end of their cigarettes. It's a sad scene. Wherever possible a room, a closet, a store-cupboard should be set aside for smokers.

Scent and aftershave pose a different problem. It's true that some people are adversely affected by strong cosmetic smells, suffering headaches and nausea, but as yet there is no evidence that *Fatale* or *Roi Soleil* can kill or maim. It's really up to users of scent and aftershave to understand that their enticing fumes constitute an invasion of others' private space, and that over-indulging in splashing it on is consequently bad manners. We haven't yet reached the stage where separate office accommodation is provided for the heavily perfumed, but the day may well come. Already in some restaurants in the United States areas are set aside for people wearing strong perfume or aftershave 'that might offend'. Until the over-aroma-ed are forcefully segregated from the rest of us, a little consideration is necessary.

Closed doors and private calls
Privacy is a two-dimensional concept. There are the times and places when we must respect the privacy of others within the office, and there are the times and places when we must

122

respect the office and not inject what is essentially a private part of our lives.

We should always be alert to occasions when our workmates are to be left in peace. If Hall or Payne has made it clear that he or she wishes to be left in peace to finish the monthly report, then that wish should be respected. If Noble has said that she doesn't want any calls for the next hour, then she should be left undisturbed. There is often a problem here, in that it is not unknown for Noble later to say: 'Yes, I know I said no calls, but I didn't expect Amalgamated Gremlins to phone – you must have realised that I wanted to speak to them.' Whatever Noble may think or say (and however important she may be), the responsibility is hers – if there were exceptions to the No Calls rule, then she should have listed them. Similarly, if Stone's door is usually open (a sign that he is happy to receive visitors or be interrupted), then we shouldn't barge in when it is closed.

But Hall, Payne, Stone, Noble and co. mustn't abuse this right to privacy. If Hall and Payne should have completed the monthly report a week ago, then they shouldn't plead ineptitude as a reason for avoiding this week's tasks. Stone can't keep his door shut all day every day, and a time will come when Noble has to accept phone calls.

The other side to privacy is that it behoves everyone in business not to bring their private lives, hobbies, affairs, moonlighting business deals and sporting interests into the office. Many companies are tolerant when it comes to using an office phone to make a private call (if it's local). Many employees take it as a sign of acceptance into the inner sanctum of office life when they are allowed to do so. Indeed, it would be unreasonable not to allow an employee to phone home if his or her partner was ill, or if there was some other family crisis. But it's a concession that is subject to immense abuse. It may be understandable that, in the middle of a fraught day, we should like to take ten minutes time out to chat on the phone to the one we love, but it isn't good business etiquette. The same condemnation has to be made of calls to find out the score at Old Trafford, wish Uncle Albert a 'happy birthday', book tickets for the ballet, or order a case of champagne. If we wish to make such phone calls from the office, then we should make a list of the calls, their destination and their length, and offer to pay for them. Better that we should log such calls than that someone else in the office does so.

For the most part, however, knowing what to keep private, when to respect someone's privacy and when to ask to be left undisturbed shouldn't really create any problems. It's all largely a matter of common sense. If in doubt, better not to knock on the door, unless there's an emergency. As to what constitutes an emergency – well, that is something that only experience can teach us. One person's four-alarm fire is another's guttering candle. Unless and until we all start wearing signs on us ('DO NOT DISTURB', 'LEAVE ME ALONE', 'NO CALLS – NOT EVEN MY MOTHER'), then we shall just have to guess when someone feels like the legendary Garbo and wants to be alone.

Sex and the workplace
All the world may love a lover, but the office world doesn't love two lovers. Of all the things that should be kept private within the workplace – love, romance, lust, sex, call it what you will – this is the one above all others. Few colleagues ever smile benignly on those who waste valuable time (and space) on an intimate personal relationship during office hours. Publicly parading our passion may shock some, amuse a few, bore many. This is yet another aspect of private life that has no place in the office.

See also Chapter 8 and Chapter 18.

CHAPTER 13

The Etiquette of Business Entertaining

Drink and dance and laugh and lie,
Love, the reeling midnight through,
For tomorrow we shall die!
(But, alas, we never do.)
DOROTHY PARKER
– *Not So Deep As a Well*

Introduction
Business entertaining is a complex subject, and it may help to
start by establishing some general principles:

1. Whether it's a party, a lunch, a trip to the theatre, a
   farewell gathering or whatever, there has to be a reason
   for the function and hopefully a purpose to it.
2. The usual rules about punctuality, apologies, dress, etc.
   apply – more on this later.
3. No one should ever be forced to attend a celebration.
4. Since, therefore, we are attending of our own volition,
   we should at least appear to be having a good time.
5. Few good parties are created spontaneously – preparation helps.
6. Whatever our own personal preferences in terms of
   what constitutes a blaster of a party, if we have been
   given the task of organising a party, we have to
   consider what others might like.
7. If we are thinking of entertaining clients and customers,
   no party at all might be preferable to a disaster.
8. If outsiders are invited to a party, someone should be

given the task of looking after them.

9. The best dinner parties, cocktail parties, business lunches, office thrashes and dinner dances are those which end with everyone wishing they would continue.

10. However beautifully organised the party, someone will get out of control and create a scene.

The first decision that we have to make in organising any sort of business entertainment is 'what sort?' Are we looking for an opportunity to meet with colleagues or customers over food and drink to discuss aspects of work? Do we want to celebrate some important event – the retirement of a valued colleague, the anniversary of the firm's foundation, Christmas, the signing of a major contract? Are we trying to oil the wheels of some protractedly squeaky negotiations? Each of these functions requires a different location, a different sort of party, a different guest list. So someone has initially to decide what sort of party is most apt.

Special care and consideration has to be given to such matters when some of the guests are from overseas. A party that may work well for our native colleagues may seem bewilderingly strange or even antagonisingly alien to visitors from other countries and other cultures. To invite Muslims to what turns out to be a drunken rave-up is obviously insulting, but it's also easy to give offence without meaning to, in terms of dress, food, location or even how guests are greeted – more on this in the relevant chapters in Part 2.

With the possible exception of the office thrash, every party or lunch has two sets of participants – hosts and guests. The role of the hosts (or hostesses) is to greet those invited, to generally oversee the event (making sure that people are at least adequately catered for and that no one is being ignored or upset), and to stay on to the bitter end, to make sure that everyone gets away safely. The role of the guests is to arrive at the appointed hour (if it's a business lunch) or a little after (if it's a more free-wheeling event, such as a cocktail party), to 'join in', not to outstay their welcome, and to show appreciation afterwards – more on this later.

It may all sound quite simple. Strange, then, that it should so often go wrong and end in tears.

Invitations

The purpose of the function being organised gives many clues as to what sort of function it should be, who should be invited and what sort of invitations would be appropriate. The more formal the occasion, the more formal the invitations. If we are considering a grand dinner dance or a ball, then we should consult specialist books on such a subject – *Debrett's Etiquette and Modern Manners* and *Debrett's Correct Form*, for example. If we are planning a business lunch, however, then the invitation will probably be made by telephone, allowing each side to check their diaries to fix a mutually convenient date. An in-house party (retirement or Christmas party) may be advertised on staff notice boards, with no need for individual invitations. Between the very formal and the very informal, there exist various types of party (cocktail, business reception) where written invitations are necessary. Most firms that print invitations are sufficiently expert in the matter to give good advice as to what is fitting.

Any invitation must contain details of who is inviting whom, to what, when and where, and perhaps some indication of the degree of formality involved; e.g. if dinner jacket or lounge suit is required attire. For guests who are less in touch with the dealings of the company acting as host, it helps to include on the invitation some indication of why this particular luncheon or cocktail party is being held – to welcome a visiting trade delegation, to mark the retirement of the Managing Director, to celebrate Fifty Glorious Years of Plastic Broom-handles. It should be abundantly clear just what it is that people are being invited to – this is especially so when food is an integral part of the occasion. Nobody wants to arrive at what turns out to be a full-blown dinner expecting nothing but *canapes*. Worse, nobody wants to arrive expecting a four course meal when all they are to be offered is peanuts.

The invitation should also indicate how and to whom the invitee should reply. 'RSVP' on the bottom of the invitation is fairly useless unless there is an address to which to write and a person at that address. Increasingly it is becoming the practice to give a name and phone number for replies, or to enclose a separate slip which the invitee fills in and returns. Some people labour long and hard over the correct wording of an acceptance or (more often) a sad declining, but only the most formal of invitations requires a similarly formal reply. If in doubt, again, it's best to consult a specialist book.

Entertaining clients and customers
The mistake to be avoided here is trying to mix business with pleasure. We shall come to business or working lunches later in this chapter, both of them perfectly valid occasions. What isn't acceptable is inviting customers to what appears to be a social celebration and then pushing them up against the wall and attempting some hard selling pitch. It happens, and it can be as much the fault of the guest as the host. As a writer, I don't often get invited to any sort of function (no tears, please), and those to which I am invited are full of other writers. It is not a pleasant sight to watch writers at, say, a BBC or publishers' function desperately touting for work. If we have invited clients to a cocktail party, then we may offer them hospitality and our thanks for their past custom, but hustling for further business must await another time and another place. A social event should be a social event.

Problems arise when a company organises a reception 'to thank our customers for their continued support over the last twelve months . . .', say, and then accidentally leaves one of those customers off the list of guests. There is sometimes the faint hope that the neglected customer won't get to hear of the reception, but bad news always travels fast. The only thing to do here is tacitly to acknowledge the mistake, and invite the neglected customer to some other get-together, perhaps a special lunch. The suggestion can then be made that 'we

128

wanted to mark our appreciation of your custom in some special way.' Even if the neglected customer sees through this ruse (and they probably will), they may still appreciate the attempt at reconciliation.

The office party

The jokes that abound about office parties fall into two categories: those concerning sexual romps and indiscretions, and those concerning drunkenly injudicious remarks to bosses and supervisors. Neither practice is to be commended, though both are understandable.

One of the ways of avoiding widespread embarrassment at and after the traditional office party is to plan some more controllable alternative. A trip to the theatre, an excursion on a river boat, or a dinner at a restaurant sets tighter parameters – there aren't any cupboards or lifts or executive washrooms to which couples can sneak for illicit joy, and the constraints of having to remain seated at a table quells some of their more rampart ardour. There is always the problem of who has to sit next to the office bore, but a dinner party can be a godsend to the less extrovert members of staff who never really look forward to a night of fuddled fondling and inebriated innuendo. Some points to be borne in mind when organising such a dinner party are:

1. Fix the time and venue early if this is a Christmas celebration. Most suitable locations are booked weeks if not months ahead, and no one wants to celebrate Christmas in early October.
2. Make sure that the price per head is not embarrassingly high for those not on high salaries.
3. Remember that 10% (or more) of the population of Britain is vegetarian (and don't let the meat eaters consume vast quantities of the vegetarian dishes 'just to see what it's like').
4. It helps if the location is well served by public transport – there will be those who do not wish to spend the night

on mineral water and those who cannot afford mini-cabs.

5. Come to a clear arrangement with the restaurant proprietor as to when the celebration must end – and then stick to the deadline.

For those who still prefer the traditional 'at home' office party, there are a number of dos and don'ts:

1. Don't get over-excited – an insult is an insult however merrily it is delivered.
2. Even if the site of the party ends up looking like the morning after the battle of Waterloo, it helps if it starts out looking welcoming and festive (six balloons sello-taped to the fax machine really aren't enough).
3. Do try to help those who are shy to have a good time. It doesn't help if a party ends up looking like the morning before the battle of Waterloo, with opposing armies confronting each other.
4. Similarly, if we are shy, we should at least try to join in the fun.
5. Don't leave all the preparations to the one or two noble souls who did it last year and the year before that and the year . . .
6. Don't leave all the clearing up to the one or two noble souls who did it last year and the year before that, and . . . (see note below).
7. Make sure that all security staff, janitors, office clean-ers and company know about the party, even if they aren't invited to it. A party that ends with a row about locking-up time doesn't go down as a good party.
8. It can help if some indication is given (on invitations or posters or however the party is publicised) as to what the purpose of the party is – to get together in an informal and friendly fashion, to mark the festive season, to enable members of the department to meet management, or whatever. If the party has an

expressed purpose, then there is (slightly) less chance of it getting wildly out of hand. There is, so to speak, a point of reference.

9. Don't force people to drink. There is nothing criminal or sinister about those who believe they can have a good time on sparkling, or even still, mineral water.

10. Remember, those who are allegedly grown-up will always find a way of making horrendous mistakes, so it's silly to pretend we can police their behaviour.

NOTE: If the staff of a particular office organised the party, then they are responsible for clearing up afterwards. How they do that is up to them. If the management organised the party, then they are responsible for clearing up. How they do that is also up to them, but it would be extremely ill-mannered if they asked the staff to do the job for them.

As to the personal behaviour of each and every one of us, that's up to the individual. Some people seem unable to attend an office party without breaking almost every social rule there has ever been. If the office party is on a Friday night (and it's wise to hold it then – much healing and forgiveness can take place over a weekend), then the usual end-of-the-week feeling will be heightened. If it's on a Saturday night, then many will have spent the day hyping themselves up and the early evening having one or two stiffeners. If it's on a Monday night, little work will be done for the rest of the week. Whenever it is, there will be drunkenness. There will be sickness in weird places. There will be ill-judged advances and ill-judged acceptances of such advances. There will be undiplomatic remarks that make 'Aside from that, Mrs Lincoln, how did you enjoy the play?' seem the epitome of tact.

Much of this will be forgiven, but there are certain things that are taken most unkindly. The office party is not the time to buttonhole the boss or head of department to tell them what we think of them, to sneak on our fellow workers, to demand a raise, to explode the myth that all is well in accounts, to confront them with the Dickensian conditions in

131

which we toil. Despite Hollywood evidence to the contrary, it isn't the time to grab the boss by the lapels and reveal our wonderful new invention/formula/plan that will rescue the company from the jaws of bankruptcy or hostile take-over. Nor is it the time to grovel before them, pleading for advancement, listing our impressive qualities and qualifications and rubbishing that little bastard Jones who couldn't organise a mutiny in a slave ship. It may be that the boss or the marketing manager opens up a conversation about the state of the company, but that isn't a signal that all protocol is to go by the board and we may establish the Revolutionary Council there and then. The boss is merely trying to show that he or she is a reasonable person, not that all authority has been relinquished or that the firm is ripe for a *coup d'etat*. If, of course, the boss invites criticism, then that's a different matter, and the boss is guilty of a breach of etiquette if he or she subsequently resents what is openly and honestly said. But the best advice is to keep all discussion on an amicable level.

If we do make the occasional mistake (mistaking the boss's husband for a bit of loose stud, or tipsily spending the odd half hour explaining to the head of accounts how cunningly we have been running a porno mail order business using the company's phone, notepaper, jiffy bags and franking machine), then we have to spend some time during the morning after deciding what to do by way of apology or recompense. The average office party sin (straightforward boorish drunkenness or a stream of Chubby Brown's riper jokes) may be best left without apology – it often doesn't help to remind people of what we did, and they certainly won't want to remind us if we can't remember what it is we're apologising for. But if we badly overstepped the mark, then it's time to take a deep breath – preferably not a garlic and whisky laden one – a couple of Rennies, and humble ourselves before whomever.

One or two words of caution here. We should always make sure of our facts before we embark on this sorry process. We should know for certain what we did wrong, and where we should lay our apology. Not only is it very confusing to the recipient of an apology if he or she has no idea why we are apologising to them, it smacks of inefficiency on our part, and we may be marked down not because of what we did but because we are clearly incompetent and ill-organised.

For gaffes of a more personal or sexual nature, see Chapter 18.

Cocktail parties (also known as Drinks Parties)

Whole books have been written about how to organise a successful cocktail party, and whole comedy routines have been based on what can go wrong at cocktail parties. For the nitty-gritty on the subject and the finer details, it's best to consult a suitable printed guide or someone who's had a great deal of experience in the art form. For the present, a few general points may be of help:

1. Invitations to a cocktail party should make clear when the party is to start and stop, and those hours may be quite short (e.g. 6.30 to 8.30).
2. Cocktail parties are good ways of returning corporate hospitality – they don't have to last long and can accommodate a large number of people.
3. Although most young people don't mind standing for a couple of hours, many old people can't – a few chairs round the room will be much appreciated.
4. Rooms in which cocktail parties are held heat up very quickly. Someone should be appointed to check the temperature from time to time.
5. If drinks are served from trays taken round the room, fine. If there is a bar where guests may replenish their drinks, then that bar must be adequately staffed – preferably by professionals.
6. Most people expect some food at a cocktail party – *canapes* or some sort of snacks.
7. The organisers of the party (the hosts) should keep an eye out for guests who have no one to talk to.

8. Cocktail parties can be messy affairs. The art of juggling a plate and a glass, cramming food into the mouth and gesticulating to impress the finer points of our conversation, is one mastered by few. It is, therefore, a good idea for the organisers to have some cleaning materials to hand.
9. Any cleaning that does have to be done, should be done as quietly and as unostentatiously as possible.
10. Guests should depart within a quarter of an hour or so of the official ending time, unless there are good (and communicated reasons) for staying longer.

It is almost unknown these days to serve cocktails at cocktail parties. Although a new generation of virulently coloured drinks has superseded the dear old Gin Fizz, White Lady and Whisky Sour, it still takes far too long to mix a cocktail for it to be a viable drink at a party. Wine is the staple liquid diet of the drinks party, and champagne for those who wish to impress, though a good wine is thought preferable to a cheap champagne by many. As at all other parties, the main purpose of the session, be it lunchtime or evening, is not to get everyone plastered, but to give guests an opportunity to relax and enjoy themselves in pleasant company. And, since there are those who are able to do just that without the aid of Bacchus, it's a good idea to have several crates of mineral water handy.

Business and working lunches

Everyone knows what a Ploughman's Lunch is, but it's much harder to describe a business lunch, though the Inland Revenue would dearly love to come up with a legally water-tight definition.

There are three sorts of business lunch: the celebratory, the working and the exploratory. The celebratory needs little explanation – it is simply a gastronomic and social way of marking some venture or contract or piece of marketing that has met with success. The working lunch (despite what the Inland Revenue may think) is just that – a lunch at which work is done, sketching out plans for the next project, discussing possible initiatives, planning tactics for a forthcoming sales pitch. The exploratory lunch is one where those sitting at table are sizing each other up, having a look to see if doing business together would be possible, wise or profitable, and trying to discover exactly what that business might be. It should be made clear to all those attending the lunch what the purpose of the meeting is. It's fine if the meal is intended as a reward for services rendered, or as thanks for business co-operation, but there is something clumsy about obviously using what should be a pleasant meal as a bribe to someone. There may be no such thing as a free lunch, but even the finest *entrecote bordelaise* sticks in the gullet if it's washed down with too many conditions and insinuations.

Whatever the reason for the lunch, much the same rules prevail. It is essential that the host is at the venue before the appointed hour. Guests should not have to wait at a restaurant that is probably unknown to them, wondering if they have made some mistake as to date, time or location. Whatever time has been fixed for the lunch, the host should be there five minutes early, to check that the reservation has been correctly made, that the table is where he or she wishes it to be, to have a brief chat with the restaurant manager about wines and the special dish of the day, and possibly to have a quick glance at the menu. If the restaurant is hitherto unknown to the host, then the menu should have been checked before the day appointed for the lunch – it's no good turning up at a restaurant to which we have invited three Vegans and a fishetarian to discover that the place we have chosen is strictly a steak and ribs joint.

Since the hosts have arrived in good time, they will be there to greet the guests when they come. If anything goes wrong, and either hosts or guests are unaccountably delayed, the usual rules regarding lateness prevail – notice of probable lateness must be communicated as early as possible, from host to guest or from guest to host, and from either to the restaurant. It is, therefore, a good idea if the host not only tells the guest where the restaurant is, but passes on the telephone number of the restaurant when the invitation is issued.

Once the party is assembled, the eating and drinking may begin. If the lunch is to be a slow-paced performance, then it may be appropriate to have a drink before moving to the table. Not many people can afford to spend the best part of half a day over lunch, however, so it's more usual to go straight to the table and order drinks there. If the menu is a large one, then it helps if the host makes some suggestions as to what might be ordered, based on his or her experiences at the restaurant. If the host doesn't know the restaurant (and it's not always a mistake to go somewhere unknown, though there are obvious risks), then it's a good idea to ask the head waiter, waiter, *maitre d'hotel*, or whoever for their recommendations. If, however, the host is well acquainted with the restaurant, then he or she may boldly step in and indicate what dishes they would recommend. To do so is not mere showing-off. It is a sign that care has been taken over the selection of the restaurant and that the host wishes to look after the guests to the best of his or her abilities.

Those of us blessed with confidence and a fountain of bibulous experience will plunge enthusiastically into the wine list. Others may prefer to receive instruction (or at least advice) from the wine waiter. Old rules and conventions about wine have changed dramatically over the last ten or twenty years. Although there's still some truth in the 'red with meat, white with fish or poultry' routine, we can afford to be a little more discerning. Some red wines can be very heavy going at lunchtime, leading inexorably to an afternoon of drowsiness. There's nothing wrong with sticking to white wine if we prefer it, whatever we are eating. Also, the European monopoly of the quality wine trade has long been a thing of the past. Australia, New Zealand, South Africa and California produce some of the finest wines in the world. One little word of caution, however – if our guests include those of sensitive political views (which usually means of a left wing persuasion), then as hosts we should perhaps avoid wines from those countries whose policies are seen to be racist, bigoted or repressive. If all our guests are of a right wing persuasion then there's nothing to worry about. Fascists will drink anything.

There is no need to be daunted by the array of cutlery in a restaurant. Usually it is made clear which knife or fork we are to use with which dish. The general rule is start from the outside (where we shall find small knife for bread and butter and soup spoon on the right, and small fork for melon or Parma ham on the left) and work in towards the plate as the meal progresses. In many restaurants the cutlery for each course appears with the dish itself. If we are really knife-and-fork illiterate, there are two ways out of what could be an embarrassing situation – wait and see how others are coping, or consult a good book on table manners.

It is the guests' duty to be appreciative of the food and drink with which they are served. It is the hosts' duty to make sure that everyone is well looked after. However earnest the conversation may be, however tight the negotiations, however detailed the plans being laid, the host should always take an occasional quick glance round the table to see if anyone appears ill at ease, thirsty, unhappy with the food in front of them or in need of a large wet sponge. The host isn't alone in all these responsibilities: they are shared by the restaurant staff. Any restaurant worth its salt and pepper will take care of its lunchtime customers, for competition is fierce in most towns and the recession has led to a mini-famine in the business lunch trade.

At the end of a meal there is sometimes a problem as to when people should depart. Each person at the meal may have a different sort of schedule in mind for the afternoon. There will be those who are eager to get back to the office where important work awaits them. There will be those who have nothing to do until sauntering to the 16.55 to Birmingham. There will be several who would like another liqueur. So some will be in a hurry to depart and others will want to spend another hour or so, pushing the crumbs up and down the white tablecloth and drawing on their cheroots. Ending the meal with coffee is often a good idea, as that provides a kind of flexi-time finale. It is perfectly in order for any guest to thank the host for the meal at any time once coffee is served and then depart. The host has to hang on to the bitter end – and has to settle the bill, of course. If it is clear that one or more guests are reluctant to move, then it is quite in order for the host to explain that he or she has to leave as they have another appointment back at the office. This should be taken by the guests as a signal that the meal is over and that the time has come for all to depart. If the guests need further prompting, then it's a good idea for the host to have one or two subtle phrases ready, such as: 'I'm heading towards the City Centre – can I offer you a lift?' or 'I'm after a taxi – would you like one, too?' If the guests still don't take the hint, then the host may leave anyway, with some kind parting remark along the lines of 'I have to go now – I'm sure they'll look after you here very well.' All it needs then is a quick word to the restaurant manager about any further expense being added to his or her account. The host has then fulfilled his or her duty – it is the guest who is at fault.

Parting parties
There are still some occasions when people leave a firm because they want to, not because they have been sacked. When a colleague retires, or moves on to riper, richer pastures, it is customary to mark the occasion by throwing a small party or at least assembling in the appropriate office to raise a glass and wish him or her well. It is up to the leaver's colleagues to decide how elaborate the farewell should be. Someone who has been with the firm for a short while may receive little more than a bunch of flowers, a record token and a bottle of wine. The whole event may take little more than five minutes. Someone who has been loyally working away for the company over decades, however, is entitled to a more extravagant celebration, a general downing of tools, perhaps even a special party.

Whatever format is deemed suitable, a little pre-thought is necessary. The 'goodbye' should suit the person departing. A shy person will not want fanfares, dinner dances and to be called upon to make a speech. Even an extrovert may not welcome a surprise party. Sensitive people may not wish to have to withstand an emotionally charged farewell. Somebody has to take on the responsibility of organising the event, however humble or elaborate it may be, and of planning a suitable gathering. Whoever that lucky person may be, it helps to keep a few basic points in mind, perhaps simply a few questions that have to be answered:

1. Where is the most appropriate venue? The office? A nearby bar? A restaurant?
2. When is the best time to hold the party? The day the person leaves? A day or two before? After they have left is almost certainly too late – nobody wants to come back to say 'goodbye'.
3. Who should be invited? Everyone connected with the departee? Just a few cronies? Management?
4. How elaborate is the occasion to be? Will there be formal speeches, reviewing the achievements of the departee while working for the company? Or should it be more informal, with some merry banter that centres on the departee's cock-ups and eccentricities?
5. If there are going to be formal speeches, who should be asked to make these speeches?
6. Is there to be a collection for a leaving present? Who's going to make the collection? Who's going to be asked to contribute?
7. Should the departee be consulted about any of these arrangements?
8. Who will see the departee safely into a taxi at the end of this emotionally draining evening?
9. Who's going to clear up when it's all over?
10. Once the collection has been made, who will have the awful task of choosing a suitable present?

Collecting money for a leaving present is a complex business. Taking an envelope round suggests that only cheques or folding money are expected – better, therefore, to take a tin or a box. There may well be those who don't wish to contribute – either out of personal animosity towards the person leaving, or because they can't afford to, or because they've only just joined the company and they've never met the person for whom the collection is being made. In each case there is a chance of causing embarrassment, so it is sometimes better if the word goes round that Firman or Smith is organising a collection and that they are, therefore, the people to see. This allows those who don't wish to contribute, for whatever reason, the chance to duck out surreptitiously.

CHECKLIST

1. All entertaining should have a purpose – even if that's little more than to have a good time.
2. No matter how much of a good time is being had by all, guests must always be looked after.
3. Business and pleasure don't often mix, and we should give notice to clients and customers if that is what we intend.
4. The traditional office party has a lot going against it.
5. Whatever species of office party we plump for, someone has to take responsibility for seeing people off the premises, etc.
6. It always helps to give people a deadline, at which time the party will cease.
7. Business lunches should be well-organised, well-sited and professionally conducted.
8. At any office-sponsored entertainment, the host must be the first to arrive.
9. People should be invited to contribute to collections for leaving presents, etc – not forced to.
10. A considerate guest knows when to leave – an inconsiderate guest has to be asked.

CHAPTER 14

Scandal, rumour and gossip

Love and scandal are the best sweeteners of tea.
HENRY FIELDING – *Love in Several Masques*

Introduction

No matter how enthusiastic we may be professionally, there are times when working in an office lacks the excitement of, say, coming third in a Latin-American Regional Dance Championship or having a letter published in a local free newspaper. And it's at such times that the worthiest among us may drop our moral standards and become prey to the seductions of office gossip. In any large office, at any given time, there is usually a rumour to be picked up, but we should resist temptation to join in the company tittle-tattle. It's a case of 'Hear no evil, see no evil, speak no evil, do no evil – or, at least, don't get found out.' Rumour is rather like the dawn – it springs up every day, many people find it thrilling and awe-inspiring, but for some it heralds the hour of execution.

We all have our moments of weakness when we join the gossiping throng, with cries of 'Did he really?', 'Surely not in the stationery cupboard!', or 'Well, she's the last person I would have suspected . . .' An occasional lapse is generally forgivable, but there are those who make a regular practice of maligning others or of spreading morale-lowering misinformation about the future outlook for the firm that employs them. Gaining a reputation as a rumour-monger or gossip is not a wise career move. For a while we may be the centre of attention at every tea-break, but sooner or later rumour reaches the wrong ears, and then there's trouble. Also, within a surprisingly short time, most colleagues tire of snide comments, innuendo, unsubstantiated accounts of

141

alleged misdemeanours, and negative speculation. To keep the tea-break audience enthralled, the gossip has to produce rumours that are more and more enthralling, more and more outrageous. It's a task that would challenge Scheherezade herself.

Sources of rumour
There are, however, some rumours which it's difficult to ignore, notably those that have some relevance to our own position within the company. More in a moment about what to do if we become the victims and subjects of rumour, but there are also those rumours about the future of the firm, about redundancies, shut-downs, mergers, take-overs, bankruptcies and all the other joys of the business world.

The difficulty about rumours such as these is that it's impossible to ignore them. If someone has heard something, or read something, or merely invented something that concerns our own professional future, there is always the sneaky feeling that we ignore it at our peril. For our own peace of mind, the best thing we can do is to try to trace the rumour back to its source. Who said it? Where did they say it? When did they say it? If it's plain old rumour these will be hard questions for the gossip to answer satisfactorily. If, on the other hand, there is some basis in truth for what is being said, then we shall find out whence the story originated. There is nothing wrong in such detective work. A little tact or diplomacy may have to be used in how it's done, however. There are obvious risks in crashing into the Managing Director's office and demanding to know 'What's all this about closing the Catford office?' or even, 'How long have you known that Grappelli was fiddling his expenses?'

If the rumour comes from a more public source – a newspaper or a snippet of television news – then there is all the more justification in seeking denial or confirmation. It is not a good idea, however, to assume that all we read or hear is true. Unless we have a remarkably close relationship with our opposite number in a rival company, we shouldn't phone to offer our condolences about their rumoured collapse simply on the basis of the odd line or two on the business pages of tabloid or broadsheet. Once the rumours have been confirmed, sympathy may be expressed if it is genuine and there is no hint of crowing about it.

The general rule is that rumour that starts from the bottom may be wishful thinking and that rumour that starts from the top may also be wishful thinking, but rumour that starts from the outside may have some truth in it as well as being wishful thinking.

Gagging gossip

If we are in a position of authority, then we are entitled to take all reasonable steps to try to stop gossip growing. If we know who's responsible for the rumour-mongering, then we can confront them with what they are doing. If there's an element of truth in the rumour, then this may not be easy. What we are then concerned with is a damage limitation exercise. It may be that the best we can do is appeal to whoever is spreading the rumour to stop, on the grounds that it is causing embarrassment or worse to the company. It may be that we consider it appropriate to take a tough stance, in the best tradition of Hollywood moguls, and threaten some kind of punitive action if the rumour persists – although there are many who adopt a 'No threats, please, we're British' approach to all their business dealings. If, however, the rumour is totally false, we may feel free to issue orders and enumerate sanctions if the guilty party doesn't comply with those orders.

For those of us who aren't in a position of authority, there are other options open to us. We may wish to display a 'holier than thou' attitude, showing that we are aware of the rumours flying around, but that we are choosing to take no notice of them. In a lot of cases, this may well make sense, though it doesn't always gain popularity. But there are occasions when the rumour is potentially harmful to the collective or the individual, and turning a deaf ear isn't the right thing to do. In such cases, one procedure is to ask the rumour-monger to

143

stop, and, if necessary, retract what they have been saying. If they don't, then we should raise the matter with the relevant authority, making sure that the culprit knows that this is what we are doing. All of this may sound more than a little prudish, but misinformation is a deadly weapon, whether it's used deliberately or negligently. People's lives have been ruined by it, and companies have gone under as a result of it.

What to do if we are the victim of rumour or gossip

Much of the above applies if we are in the unhappy position of being the victims of rumour or gossip. For a while we may be tempted to ignore it, worried perhaps that our denial may appear too forceful – back to the 'protesting too much' syndrome. In general, however, it's best to step in quickly. Rumour-mongering can be like a drug in many ways – the longer people are allowed to indulge in it, the harder it becomes for them to give up. And, although there may be the fear that by contradicting the rumour we are actually giving it some kind of validity, our silence would in most cases be interpreted as proof that there was some truth in the rumour.

If we don't know where the rumour is coming from, or if our attempts to scotch it are ineffective, then we have to take more serious action. We have to go to a superior and explain to him or her what is happening – this is based on the assumption that the rumour is ill-founded, but it may be the right thing to do even if it isn't. Seeing our superior gives us the opportunity to put our side of the matter in our own way, at our own time, without the histrionics of the 'oh, yes, you did' – 'oh, no, I didn't' session that would almost certainly take place if we waited until summoned, with the rumour-monger, to our superior's presence.

If none of the above has the desired effect of stifling the gossip, then we may ask our superior to make sure that something is done about it, we may bring in association or union help, or we may consider legal action. In many cases merely telling our superiors that we are considering legal action may convince them that they should themselves do something to circumvent this. Few firms enjoy the prospect of formal litigation between two of their employees – it creates very bad publicity. But, always remember, we should never threaten any action that we are not prepared to take.

One of the best courses of action if we are the victim of rumour is to consult with a colleague whose opinion and advice we really trust. Often, in the stress caused by being the subject of rumour, we don't think clearly, and the best courses of action may well be ones that we have not considered. A friend has a less emotional perspective on the matter, may better judge what's really happening, may know that the wisest thing to do is to let the whole affair blow over, or may offer to intervene for us.

And a final point – if we work in an atmosphere where rumour and gossip appear to go unchecked, then something needs to be done for everyone's sake.

CHAPTER 15

Correspondence

'That's a rather sudden pull up, ain't it, Sammy?' inquired Mr Weller.
'Not a bit of it,' said Sam; 'she'll vish there wos more, and that's the great art o' letter writin'.'
CHARLES DICKENS – *Pickwick Papers*

Introduction

Business correspondence is one of the great growth industries of modern times. Every day mail floods into most offices – a lot of it unnecessary, a lot of it unsolicited, a lot of it badly drafted or wrongly addressed. But among all the rubbish there are those items of correspondence that are of vital importance, and we disregard the mail or throw it straight into the bin at our peril. Because so much of it is dross, the well-written, relevant, correctly addressed, elegantly expressed letter stands out like a pearl among plastic beads, like the one good joke in a box of crackers.

So, pearl or bead, each letter we receive has to be scrutinised with enough care to make sure that we don't throw away something that really matters. It's tempting to take one look at the postmark, the letterhead, the first line and then crumple it and hurl it at McKinley or Lynn in the hope that they'll respond and we can spend a few happy minutes in missile combat. The temptation has to be resisted. If we are lucky enough to have a secretary or a PA, then the initial weeding process will have been done for us. If not, then we must do it ourselves. An awful lot of time has to be wasted in reading correspondence that has already wasted someone else's time in its writing.

The bombardment of business missives has increased as

competition has intensified, as recessions have made people more and more desperate to find a job or sell a product or gain a contract, as new markets have opened and old ones have closed, and as new methods of communication have appeared. 'Correspondence' used to mean simply those manilla and white envelopes that thudded into the mailbox or mail room every morning. Now it includes faxes, and great wodges of jiffy bags or huge packets that are brought to reception every five minutes by sweating, helmeted couriers – men with trousers that squeak even in dry weather. There is never a moment in the working day when we can truly say that we have dealt with the day's correspondence.

All of which indicates that any letter or fax or packet that we send must be for some legitimate purpose, and that purpose should be readily and easily apparent to the recipient. It is poor business practice to send a letter so obtusely written that the poor reader has to plod through three or four hundred words before discovering that it's a request to keep a pot plant on a desk or confirmation of a meeting that has been arranged. The nitty-gritty of most letters could be expressed in five lines at the most. The end of business communication should be efficiency, not the Nobel Prize for Literature. If we send business letters full of metaphors and allegories, stuffed with surmise and similes, crammed with anecdotes and 'by the ways', then the impression we shall give is that we haven't enough work to do – and that's an impression that reflects badly on us and the company for whom we work.

Given, however, that this deluge of mail will continue – and there are few signs that it won't – we have to find ways of dealing with it. There will be (or should be) a standard office practice for handling mail and deciding what should be filed where and what should happen to the junk. We need to have, alongside that practice, a system of our own. This system need not be elaborate, but it should enable us to deal with the urgent mail swiftly, to keep the less urgent mail sufficiently to hand so that it doesn't disappear into the office limbo never to be acknowledged, and to pass mail on to the relevant department at once if it isn't for us. This is why the stick-on note was invented. Even in the mad world of business there is a purpose for almost everything.

The noble (but not Nobel) art of letter-writing

In the good old days there were very strict rules about letter-writing. Some of these rules or conventions still apply, mainly those to do with how to open and close a letter. Others have long fallen into disuse. There are those who consider it a mark of extra consideration to hand-write a letter, a sign that it hasn't simply been dictated (or even delegated) to someone else, but the alleged decline in personal handwriting means that most people would prefer something produced by a typewriter or word processor. It is still, however, a mark of respect to hand-write letters of congratulation or condolence. The hideous and confusing abbreviations of 'ult.' and 'inst.' have happily all but disappeared. Anyone who uses them nowadays probably uses a quill pen. The unctuous verbiage of the good old days ('We have the honour to beg to inform you, as our most esteemed customer . . .') is now rightly ridiculed. Such letters were always repellently hypocritical and few people want to do business with Uriah Heep and Co. We no longer live in the world of sealing wax and uniformed telegram boys.

The purpose of business letter writing (as of all other forms of correspondence) is to relay or solicit information in the clearest, shortest and most relevant way. The first question to be answered is 'Is this letter necessary?' If it isn't, we shouldn't send it. The second question is 'What sort of paper is appropriate?' There is no point in using an A4 sheet of headed notepaper if the letter consists of a single sentence. It's a waste of paper and it looks silly. If it's an internal letter, it doesn't need company heading, though we should indicate which department it comes from. If it's going to an outsider, then a piece of headed A5 paper will suffice if it's a short letter.

Some of us have moments of concern as to how we should head a business letter. Do we put 'Dear Lionel'? or should it be 'Dear Mr Hampton'? The answer is that often it would be better to put 'Dear Lionel Hampton' instead if we are writing to someone we have not met. This is another change from the good old days. To use first name and family name is less formal and less impersonal than 'Mr' and family name, but isn't crudely over-friendly. Once we have met the addressee, or once we have already exchanged letters, or if the correspondence has been initiated by 'Lionel' addressing us by first name, then we can drop the family name.

If we don't know to whom we should address the letter (e.g. if it is of a speculative nature or if it's a letter of complaint to a firm), then the best thing to do is to telephone the firm concerned and find out. If the firm doesn't want to divulge this information, then we may have to end up by heading our letter 'Dear Mountebank Corporation of Thurrock' or whatever. It is still acceptable to head letters 'Dear Sir or Madam', but it suggests that we haven't taken the trouble to find out whom we're writing to, and 'Madam' has old-fashioned or vice-like connotations.

How we head the letter may dictate the general tone. 'Dear Ella' suggests that the letter should be reasonably cordial as well as businesslike – unless, of course, it's a letter of complaint or bitter recrimination towards someone with whom we've crossed swords many times before. 'Dear Sir Charles' augurs a modicum of respect, even in our classless society. If we are writing to an archbishop, an earl or a foreign dignitary, then we should consult a book that specialises in such matters. (One small word of warning here – before following the advice of any book on letter-writing, we should check that it is a recent work, otherwise we may well find ourselves back in the land of ult. and inst.)

The way we begin the letter will dictate how we sign off. The old conventions still apply here. If we have started the letter with 'Dear Sir' or 'Dear Madam', then we should end with 'Yours faithfully' or 'Yours truly'. If we have started with 'Dear Sarah' or 'Dear Ms Vaughan' then we should end with 'Yours sincerely', though the phrase is brusquely dismissed by the OED as 'a stereotyped formula used in concluding a letter'. Again, if we are writing to the Queen or the Lord Chief Justice or the President of the United States, then we should consult an appropriate authority. If we have opened the letter with 'Dear Glenn Gray' or 'Dear Jeanette MacDonald', then we should sign with our full name, first and family. If we opened with 'Dear Glenn' or 'Dear Jeanette', then we sign the letter with just our first name, though it is essential to type both first and family name below the signature.

Often secretaries or PAs sign letters for their bosses, inserting the phrase 'pp Ann Southern' or whoever below their own signature. The letter's 'pp' stand for the Latin words *per procurationem*, which simply means 'on behalf of'. There is nothing wrong with this practice. It is usually understood to mean that the boss was out of the office when the time came to sign the letter, that the office is a busy place, and that the secretary or PA has the total trust of his or her boss. Care should be exercised in some cases, however. The more awesome, the more dignified, the more powerful the addressee, the more it behoves the boss to sign the letter personally and the less appropriate it is to have a secretary 'pp' it.

In the world of business it is a cliche that 'time is money'. Folding dozens of sheets of A4 paper for a mail shot can take quite a bit of time, and it's understandable that some firms prefer to place even a single sheet of A4 paper unfolded in an A4 envelope. However, more and more people are conscious of the limits to the planet's resources. An A4 envelope is a mighty thing – there aren't many of them to the tree. Nobody minds unfolding a letter, but they may resent what they regard as environmental profligacy. It may be perfectly fine to send several sheets of A4 unfolded, but one, two or three sheets fit more snugly, after one or two folds, in a smaller envelope. Not only that, they arrive in better shape. A single piece of A4 paper in an A4 envelope usually arrives in a battered and crumpled condition, which doesn't create a good impression.

151

Replying to letters

Junk mail needs no response – even if we've bothered to read it. Unsolicited mail in general may have to wait its turn for an answer, but it is still considered bad manners by most people if we do not reply to our mail. If we wish to make a phone call instead of writing a letter, that is perfectly acceptable in most cases. Where we need particularly to acknowledge an order, a contract or a complaint, then a letter should be sent. In general terms, the sooner the letter is written and sent, the better. There are many who judge a company and its staff by the speed and efficiency with which they deal with their mail.

Using company headed notepaper

Whenever we send a business letter we should send it on company notepaper. To do otherwise seems sloppy or suggests that the company is short of funds. Company headed paper should not, however, be used for the following:

1. Letters of a personal nature. This is a difficult area to define. Often we write letters of congratulation or condolence both as private individuals and as representatives of the company for whom we work. In such cases, company paper is appropriate. If we are writing purely as a private individual, however, we should use private paper.
2. Any letters that express private opinions – e.g. political views. To link our company with a party political opinion or policy is a breach of business etiquette. This rule also applies to letters that seek to raise funds for charities, unless the fund-raising is sponsored by our company and is being carried out in their name.
3. Letters which express views and opinions markedly different from those of the company.
4. Letters of application for jobs with other companies. It is not that this will necessarily give a bad impression, it is simply a matter of courtesy to the company for whom

152

we work. And if we are seen to be discourteous to our present employer, then a potential future employer may have doubts about us.

5. Letters to the media about our job or our company or related topics that express personal opinions. We may passionately believe in the proposed merger with Swizzles, but writing to *The Times* on company paper to this effect is looking for trouble.

6. Any letters that don't relate to company matters.

Second thoughts

For every piece of work there is a deadline, and that means pressure to get matters dealt with quickly. There are occasionally those letters or memos or faxes that require a little extra thought, however. If, after the first draft of a tricky piece of correspondence or a major complaint or a letter of resignation, we have time to sleep on it then we may hit upon a better way of dealing with whatever problem we face. Once a letter or fax has been sent, there's no way we can intercept it – it will arrive at its destination. Second thoughts are often better on those business letters written in anger. If we have sent a letter, and subsequently wish we hadn't, then the only thing we can do is to contact the person to whom we've sent the letter (before or after they receive it), explain how we now feel and offer whatever apology we wish to make. There are stories of people emerging from such a situation in a better position *vis a vis* their correspondent than they were in before they sent the regretted letter – but there are also stories of monumentally awful repercussions. It's best not to send such a letter in the first place.

Before sending a letter of complaint, it's a good idea to sit back and take stock of the situation that has prompted us to wish to complain. Here it helps to ponder over a few questions:

1. Is it appropriate to complain about this matter?
2. What sort of complaint should be made? A demand for

153

recompense? For an apology? For another meal/ delivery/machine?

3. Is the complaint actually justified – or are we being too sensitive?

4. Are we being too proud, too high and mighty? Paranoid?

5. Are we making a mountain out of a molehill?

6. Are we complaining to the right person?

7. Are we complaining in the right way?

8. Are we looking for the solution to a problem? Or are we hoping for a bare-knuckle fight?

9. Are there colleagues or superiors with whom we should consult before making this complaint?

10. What sort of results might our complaint produce? And are these likely results what we are seeking?

If we're uncertain about any of these points, then it's time for second thoughts.

Letters to the media
Great care should always be taken before going public in our correspondence. Most companies have rules (written or unwritten) as to who is allowed to contact radio, TV and newspapers about which issues. The proliferation of leaks to the press has led some companies to keep a closer eye on documents and a tighter control on information. Clearly, selling or giving away secret or private information from a company is the breach of etiquette that passeth all others. But there are also minor matters – issues within the company that we think should be brought to the public's attention, or wise and witty observations that we're bursting to make.

No matter how witty, no matter how wise, we have to contain our desire for a few minutes' fame, and take our suggestions to the right department or person within our organisation. This applies even when we are merely replying to an article or letter already published in the press, or to the views of someone else already expressed in an interview on radio or TV. As employees of a company, we do not, as individuals, have an untrammelled right to reply, unless we have been attacked personally – and even then it is probably better at least to consult with our employers about the most suitable kind of response. And, as is the case with all correspondence, there should be a clear purpose to any letter, phone call, fax or whatever to the media.

Whenever anyone contacts the media from a company, it's best if someone else checks what is being done and said. In some cases the legal department may wish to keep a watching brief. In others, the publicity or press departments need to know. Even if someone has the authority to deal directly with the media, embarrassment (and sometimes worse) is avoided if heads are put together before issuing a press release or writing to the *Financial Times*.

Finally, we have to use our imaginations when contacting the media. We may have a very clear idea as to what the purpose of our letter is, or why we're consenting to be interviewed – it's to give the company some good publicity, or to refute some dastardly allegation made by a wicked journalist, or to add our support to some informal campaign that's running. It is, however, quite possible that the media may find some other use for our letter or personal appearance – twisting our words to achieve exactly the opposite of what we had hoped for. Before making any contact with the media, second, third and even fourth thoughts are often advisable.

Memos and faxes – their uses and abuses

Some people are very good at sending memos. They know just how to word them, who to send them to, how long to make them, and how often to send them. Others make a dreadful mess of the whole memo business – too many, too often, too impersonal, too wordy. Memos shouldn't be like daily battalion orders – sent impersonally to every department every day, piling on extra work to all and sundry, and griping about poor performance and targets not reached. Just because a memo is (or should be) short, it doesn't have to be curt. A good memo should leave its recipient with a feeling of 'Thank God, Tessie reminded me of that', or 'Well, I'm glad everyone upstairs appreciated the hard work that went into July's sales drive.'

To pass on thanks or congratulations, a letter is usually better than a memo, simply because it's more personal. To make criticisms (if one or two members of a department are being picked out), a letter is always better than a memo – and an interview is often better than a letter. Memos are good for passing on general information to the members of an office or department – in much the same way that some people use circulars. They are very good when stuck or pinned to the top of a bundle of documents – everyone reads the top page of a bundle of documents. Not everyone stops to peruse the notices on a bulletin board, however, so we should never assume that, just because we stuck a memo on the office wall, everyone has read it. It's strange that notices should be called 'notices', when so many take so little notice of them. If news is important, it should be carefully relayed. There's a lot that can be said for memos, but there's also a lot that can't be said on them.

Faxes are wonderful things, as fax machine salespeople never stop reminding us. Being able to send copies of documents, graphs, pictures, diagrams almost instantaneously anywhere in the world is a great boon to the business world. Those of us without a fax number on our business cards feel somehow out of the mainstream of life, marooned in our lonely little backwaters that rely on the phone and the post.

But the trouble with faxes is that they cannot help seeming a little peremptory. They arrive by machine, spat out into the middle of an office, often unsolicited, occasionally unwelcome, and they have to sit there on their pile, waiting for someone to come and collect them. There is an aura of the Battersea Dogs' Home about faxes. So it's sometimes better to phone to announce the impending arrival of a fax, and that may mean that there's no need to send a fax at all – for the trouble is that there are some who abuse the fax system. They send a fax instead of making a phone call. Admittedly, when a line is engaged it's tempting to send a fax so that we can consider that we have finished with that particular piece of business and race on to the next. But if we're sending a fax instead of phoning, then what we have produced is the equivalent of a phone monologue, a one-sided phone call, where we say everything and the other party says nothing. It isn't possible to fax a conversation.

CHECKLIST

1. Don't indulge in unnecessary correspondence.
2. All communication should be as brief as possible, because
3. All communication has to be dealt with.
4. But a two line letter on a piece of A4 paper looks ridiculous, so we must make the paper smaller, not the letter bigger.
5. We should check how to head and sign off any letter.
6. Private letters should not be sent on company notepaper.
7. It often pays to have second thoughts about the wording, or even the sending, of a letter or fax.
8. We should check with the appropriate authority within the company before we send any letters to the media.
9. It is permissible to send good news as well as bad.
10. Faxes are wonderful things, but don't always seem so at 17.25 on a Friday evening.

CHAPTER 16

Telephone etiquette

Well, if I called the wrong number, why did you answer the phone?

JAMES THURBER – caption to cartoon in *New Yorker*

Introduction

Phone users fall into one of two categories – those who love the telephone and those who hate it. Phone-lovers grab the instrument hungrily, dial eagerly, cradle the receiver between shoulder and chin, doodle happily on a notepad while conversing, spend hours talking and hang up reluctantly. They are completely happy when talking to anyone, and are often oblivious as to how their call is being received at the other end. They would happily spend all day on the phone. Phone-haters have to psych themselves to make a call in the first place. They reach for the dreaded machine with trembling hand, dial hesitantly but often misdial (so that they have to start again), flinch when they hear the ringing tone and are lost for the correct words when someone answers. Their clammy hands shake while holding the receiver, and they can do little but gaze blindly into the distance while talking. To them making or taking a phone call is only marginally less terrifying an experience than a visit to the dentist.

In business terms, those who fall within the first of these two categories see the phone as an end in itself, and may jam the switchboard for hours, while those who fall within the second category seem to understand that the phone is merely a means of communicating with another human being. Somewhere between the two categories there should be a phone zone where callers are relaxed enough not to transmit tension, but sufficiently conscious that the receiver may have other things

159

to do so that they don't take up an entire morning or afternoon.

Whichever category we fall into, each and every one of us should try to cultivate a pleasant phone manner – not too hearty, not too distant. This applies whether we are making or taking a call. We need to speak clearly. We need to adopt certain basic phone practices – giving our name, department, number, almost as though we were being taken prisoner of war. We need to concentrate on what is being said, by us or by the person at the other end of the line. We need to remember, above all, that a phone call often gives an outsider their first (and perhaps their only) impression of an office, a department, or an entire company.

First impressions

Picking up a phone when it rings and saying 'Yes?' or 'What?' is not good manners and doesn't impress. Nor does giving the name of the firm or department in a voice that implies that the caller is a thorough nuisance who could not have picked a more inconvenient time to phone. Nor does picking up the phone and continuing a conversation we are having with someone else before deigning to speak to whoever is on the other end of the line. We do not have to shriek with enthusiasm or give the impression that we have been sitting by the phone all day, longing for this particular call.

The way we answer the phone reveals a great deal. It tells the caller something about the sort of people our company employs, but it may go much further than that. It will probably set the tone for the whole conversation – or at least profoundly influence it. A caller who is already in a bad mood will not be soothed if our response is grudging or discourteous. A caller who is having difficulty obtaining information may well give up in disgust if we treat his or her call with bored disdain. A caller who has something to offer that may be of benefit to our company may also hang up if it sounds from our tone of voice that we couldn't care less.

It can be an interesting experience to sit in the reception

area of any firm, within earshot of the person operating the telephone switchboard. The best of such operators are real professionals, ceaselessly answering calls and redirecting them to the appropriate recipients. No matter how many times per minute they have to answer the phone, they manage to make each 'Good morning . . . Preagers and Rabins . . . how may I help you?' sound fresh and polite, however bathetic the phrase that they have been instructed to use. Sloppy operators, on the other hand, sound rude, fed up, and as though the last thing their firm wants is any contact with the outside world. The difference between the two is fundamental. The first inspire hope and confidence: the second make the caller feel like replacing the receiver as quickly as possible. The first make us believe that we are in touch with a happy, efficient, go-ahead company: the second make us feel as though we have phoned just in time to catch the terminal moments in the life of the firm we have phoned.

As in so much of business life, a few basic rules about making and taking calls may be helpful:

1. Even if nature has not blessed us with the pipes of a Gielgud or Dench, we should try to make our voice sound clear and pleasant. It should appear that we are paying attention.
2. We should identify who and what and possibly where we are the moment we answer.
3. We should listen carefully to what the caller has to say to us.
4. We should take especial care in noting the name of the caller, the name of the person he or she wishes to speak to, and any other names that crop up during the conversation.
5. We should be patient and tolerant on the phone. If the caller has not sufficiently prepared what he or she has to say, then we have to give them a chance to make up for that.
6. If the caller has come through to the wrong extension,

or the call isn't for us, we shouldn't give the impression that we think that is the caller's fault – or anyone else's fault, for that matter. There has simply been a misunderstanding.

7. We should not fight fire with fire (more on handling unwanted calls later in this chapter). If whoever phones us is spitting and snarling, we should turn the other ear.

8. If we have to interrupt the caller (for his or her own good – to redirect them to someone who can be more helpful to them, say), then we should interrupt as politely as possible.

9. We should lie as little as possible on the phone (more on this later in the chapter).

10. If we promise to call back, we should keep this promise.

A very similar set of rules applies when we make the call. Here, to the above, we can add:

1. At all times we should remember that we have chosen the time this particular call has been made. It may be very convenient for us to speak for half an hour or more. It may not be convenient for the person we have called.

2. We should have prepared the gist of what we wish to say.

3. We should remember that, no matter how justifiably furious we may be, the likelihood is that the phone will not be answered by the person who has made us angry.

4. Being put through to the wrong extension is not the fault of the person who answers on that extension.

5. Few people welcome business calls thirty seconds before going-home time.

At all times, whether making or taking the call, we should

remember that we are merely transient representatives of the firm we work for, even if it says 'Chief Executive' on the door to our office. How we sound will decide how others rate our company. It pays, therefore, to make our calls short and to the point (but not brusque), to know what we wish to say, to time them when they will be least unwelcome, and never to make them when our minds are elsewhere and we're trying to deal with something else at the same time.

Telephone lies

In almost all cases honesty is the best policy on the telephone, though the temptations to lie (when no one can see us and we haven't yet identified ourselves) are enormous. The trouble is that most accustomed telephone users have themselves been subject to similar temptations. We are all poachers turned gamekeepers here. We know all the tricks. We know when we are being fobbed off with lame excuses – because we've used exactly the same excuses.

A classic case is when we are acting as a buffer between the caller and someone within our office who may not wish to speak to this caller – and often this someone in our office will be our boss. The caller asks to speak to 'Ms London', and we say (to keep Ms London's options open), 'I don't think she's in the office right now.' This is a fairly stupid answer anyway, as it implies that the office is about half a mile long and we'd normally need field glasses to check the occupants. So we cup our hand over the mouthpiece of the phone and hiss to Ms London, 'It's Mr McKinley – are you in or out?' And Ms London (surprise, surprise) says she will speak to Mr McKinley. So then we have to take our hand off the mouthpiece and say, 'Ms London is in the office – I'm putting you through to her.' Now, unless he is a complete numskull, Mr McKinley will guess that Ms London was in the office all the time, and we were vetting his call for her. So, the next time Mr McKinley rings, he won't believe us if we say that Ms London is out of the office. It's all a bit like the spy planes in the old Cold War. Neither side admitted they were using such wicked machines, but both sides knew they were.

Phone calls cost a great deal of money. It isn't fair, therefore, to inform a caller that we 'won't keep you one moment' if we know that the poor caller is going to have to listen to forty choruses of Scott Joplin's *The Entertainer*, or Vivaldi's *Four Seasons* played twenty times over on a one note synthesiser. Better to be truthful – waiting only makes most people cross. If, however, we admit that there will be a long wait and suggest that we get someone at our end to call back, then we have to keep this promise, even if it transpires that that someone has disappeared for the afternoon.

Shunting calls to an innocent colleague simply because we don't want to have to deal with them is a shabby trick, unfair to caller and colleague alike. Again, it may be very tempting when we've had to deal with the caller for five long minutes, but we have to be honest, tell them we can't help and neither can anyone else, and politely extract ourselves from the pointless conversation.

The only telephone lie that usually works is when we say 'I'm sorry, I'm afraid there's no one here at the moment who can help you . . .' It works because the caller cannot prove that there is – whatever he or she may suspect. But it's a lie of limited life, for the caller will either demand 'Well, when will there be somebody there who can help?' or will ring back anyway.

Handling unwanted calls

Some of us believe that the telephone was invented for the deranged, the obsessive and the unlovable. Alexander Graham Bell little knew what he was starting when he played with his taut piece of string and two empty yoghurt pots all those years ago. But the police and phone-in programmes on the radio and almost every business in the land know that telephone lines are always buzzing with unwanted calls from incomprehensible callers. Out there are all these extraordinary people, running up astronomical bills and wasting hours and hours of precious time. How wonderful it would be if we could tell them what to do. But we can't. The unwanted call will be with us for life.

Once it has become clear that we are dealing with an unwanted phone call, it's tempting to slam the receiver down or wickedly pass on the call to an unsuspecting colleague. Though very understandable, both courses of action should be avoided. Unwanted callers often ring back if cut off in full flow, and our poor colleagues will almost certainly guess who passed the call on, and then we'll get all their unwanted calls put through to our extension.

We have instead to listen carefully (but not protractedly) to every unwanted call to establish:

1. Is it a call that should genuinely be put through to someone else?
2. How best to bring the call to a speedy but reasonable polite end?

For some of us, this is an occasion for the telephone lie – 'I'm sorry, I think you've been put through to the wrong extension . . . No, I'm afraid I don't know whom you should speak to . . . No, there really isn't anybody in this office who deals with problems of that nature . . .' and then we sign off with a general and genuine-sounding mutter of regret that we are not able to help. If the caller won't accept our well-mannered brush-off, then we may have to resort to other methods. An approach that a business partner of mine often uses to good effect, when her ear has been assailed for too long by a caller, is: 'Look, this call must be costing you a great deal of money. I think we should stop talking right now. Thank you so much for calling . . . Goodbye.' It doesn't always work, but it does sometimes, and it registers a kind concern for the caller.

Whatever method we adopt in dealing with unwanted calls, in the final resort we have to be firm in our resolve to bring the call to a civilised but definite end.

The answer-phone (however we spell it) – a curse or a blessing?

For most busy people, the answering-machine has come as a boon. For the small business, it provides an extra pair of ears to deal with incoming calls when the limited number of staff are already busy. For large businesses it can sift incoming calls, suggesting which departments or extension numbers are best suited to deal with any particular enquiry. For all businesses it can provide a twenty-four hour a day, non-stop point of contact with the rest of the world, taking those calls that come in late at night or early in the morning when we mere humans are all crammed into our commuter transport.

The drawbacks of answering-machines are obvious. Apart from those kind souls who leave a message to say that they will phone again in an hour or two's time, most callers leave their own telephone number in the expectation that we shall phone them. There's nothing ill-mannered about such supposition, unless the call is solely to their advantage, or it concerns a matter of which we have no prior knowledge whatsoever, or, perhaps, if it's a long distance or international call. But usually an answering-machine means higher phone bills for its owner.

It helps enormously if the receiving message left on the answering-machine is brief, informative and well-organised. There are few things more depressing in business life (save redundancy, bankruptcy or being the victim of fraud) than calling a number only to hear, for the umpteenth time that morning, some garbled comedy routine that takes several precious minutes to say that 'I'm out' – whoever 'I' may be. Any receiving message on an answering-machine should contain at least the following information:

1. The number that has been called.
2. The name of the person or persons who would normally be available on that number.
3. When it will be possible to reach a real live human being on that number.

166

Similarly, any incoming message should be well-organised. It's no good calling and not at least half-expecting an answering-machine and therefore having nothing prepared for that eventuality. Not many of us are blessed with the ability to extemporize coherently, wittily, accurately and comprehensively. So we should spend a couple of minutes thinking about what we shall say to the machine – it shouldn't be all that different from what we shall say to a human being, and then make sure that any message we have to leave on the machine contains at least the following information:

1. The name of the person calling.
2. The name of the person he or she wished to speak to.
3. The date and time of the call.
4. A very brief description of what the call is about.
5. An honest indication of how important it is to establish direct contact – I have a colleague who signs off messages he leaves on my machine with such phrases as 'medium urgent'. It may sound strange, but it does help.
6. Any details of when the caller may phone again – such information to be adhered to – it is ill-mannered to say we shall phone again at two-thirty, and then not do so.*
7. As few jokes as are possible – unless they are very good ones.

   * NOTE: There are some people who phone at, say, eleven in the morning to say they will be phoning at three in the afternoon. In some exceptional cases this might narrowly be justifiable, although it seems a long-winded way of conducting business. What isn't justifiable, or excusable, is not subsequently phoning at three in the afternoon.

One thing that has to be done is to take note of the messages left on the machine. Whether callers have said they will

167

phone back or not, we need to keep a record of who called us and when and what about. How we best organise this is a matter of business efficiency rather than business etiquette.

The mobile phone

No matter how scorned by those of us who feel we can't really afford one, no matter how comically portrayed by TV or radio comedian, the mobile phone (or its little distant relation – the pager) is a boon. True, if our own office knows we have one it means we are never truly free, but that's a small price to pay for being able to deal with important business matters while on the train, while waiting at the bus stop, when our flight back has been delayed for several hours, or when we have sneaked off to Wimbledon for the afternoon.

Owners of mobile phones must remember, however, that they are holding a small chunk of electronic engineering, not wielding the sceptre of power. A mobile phone exists for us to talk and listen to other people, not to provide an entire railway coach or reading room at the library with a karaoake performance of 'How to Succeed in Business'. Not everyone at the supermarket checkout wants to know how negotiations are progressing with Loss and McVay.

One of the blessings of the mobile phone, from the point of view of the person calling a mobile phone, is that we don't have to worry about making a call at an inappropriately late hour, as the possessor of the mobile phone can always turn it off when he or she doesn't want any more calls.

Since calls to and from mobile phones are expensive, however, we should bear in mind all that applies to making a call to an answering-machine, and always be businesslike and brief. And there are places where mobile phones are expressly not welcome. 'Some publicans are wary of mobile phones,' says a Cellnet booklet. 'Best to switch off.' The problem is that users of mobile phones are often the gadget's worst enemies, in their desperate attempts to convince the rest of the world that they are living in the fastest of fast lanes twenty-four hours a day. They would have us believe that they are so busy, they even have to make phone calls while they are brushing their teeth.

Deflecting and defusing

From time to time tempers are lost in the great world of business. Irascible calls are not unknown on the telephone, but no matter how grave the provocation, none of us should stoop to rudeness. If we are the victims of such behaviour, there are sadly no fool-proof ways of dealing with rudeness on the telephone. Prevention is always better than cure, so the first thing we have to do is to make sure that we are never the cause of invective or personal remarks. Some people are extremely tolerant on the phone, others among us have to sweat and sweat to exercise what patience we have. If the caller starts to be uncivil, then we are entitled to point this out to him or her, and this is probably the best thing to do. It's best not to do it snappily or waspishly, and never threateningly – there's nothing a bad-tempered caller likes better than the sniff of combat in the air.

If we've pointed out that we believe the caller is being rude and this hasn't calmed him or her down, then we are at liberty to tell the caller that we are (reluctantly) going to have to put the phone down, and that we hope that it will be possible to have a reasonable conversation at another time. We should then put the phone down – not hang on to see what effect this has. Dealing with haughty or impolite callers is very much like dealing with naughty children – if we say we are going to do something, then we have to do it, even though we haven't made what we said seem like a threat.

What we shouldn't do, no matter how much we'd like to, is pass the offending caller on to someone else. If the caller is making threats, however, or is being intimidating or offensive, then we should let a superior know, or at least look for support from a colleague once the call is over. In exceptional circumstances (hopefully never to do with business) we may wish either to record the conversation or ask someone to listen on an extension. If we do this, we should inform the caller that this is happening.

CHECKLIST

1. The telephone is not a weapon, but a means of communication.
2. A phone call is often the first contact an outsider has with a company, and on how the call is conducted much may depend.
3. No matter how busy or bored we are, we should attempt to sound pleasant and to speak clearly when on the phone.
4. When we call others, we should consider whether we are calling at a convenient time.
5. Honesty is usually (but not always) the best policy on the phone.
6. Phone calls do not come cheap.
7. It is usually (but not always) possible to end an unwanted phone call by being firm but polite.
8. People leaving messages on answer-phones should speak slowly and clearly.
9. Mobile phones should be used with discretion, not flaunted like fashion on a catwalk.
10. It isn't fair to pass an unwanted phone call on to someone else unless it really is for them.

CHAPTER 17

Meetings

> Meetings that do not come off keep a character of their own. They stay as they were projected.
>
> ELIZABETH BOWEN – *House in Paris*

Introduction

One of the greatest sins in the business world is to summon or convene a meeting for which there is no reason. Some people love meetings and are never happier than when sitting round a table, smiling, nodding, frowning and wasting other people's time. But many of us loathe meetings – the prolonged wait for latecomers, the unnecessary formality and pomposity, the repetitive speeches and bitty arguments, the knowledge (as we tick each near-interminable item off the agenda) that Franklin or Whiteman will have a couple of irrelevant matters to raise under 'Any Other Business', and that we shall be lucky if we catch the 21.30. Life is short – it should be sweet. Meetings add little to the quality of existence.

No meeting, therefore, should take place unless there is a good reason for it. It should be well-planned, with careful attention paid to the number of people invited to attend, what should and shouldn't be included on the agenda, the length of time necessary to cover that agenda, how many meetings those invited or commanded to attend have already suffered in the recent past.

However keen we are to convene a meeting, we must remember that those we invite are being taken away from some other task. If they leave our meeting feeling that we have wasted their time, then we have done them and ourselves a disservice. This is true whether the meeting is an internal

171

one, with no outsiders invited, or one that includes representatives of other departments or companies. The bigger (or the longer) the meeting, the more we should be sure that it is completely necessary and that we can justify all invitations to it.

Clearly there is a huge range of meetings – from the small, informal, hastily convened putting-heads-together in the department, to the large conference or grand series of talks that involves representatives of government, trade delegations and heads of major industries. The rules governing the way meetings are run and how we should behave during them do not vary greatly. All meetings should be efficient. No meetings should degenerate into mud-slinging or haughty aloofness. Everyone should come away from any meeting feeling that it has been worthwhile.

Preparation
Every meeting has an organiser, a chairperson, a convener. If we are calling a meeting, and taking responsibility for organising it, then there are a number of matters that we must attend to long before that meeting takes place.

Firstly, we have to decide who should attend. Some people will attend as of right – they appear whether we want them or not. Some should be invited, out of courtesy or because their input is needed. Some may be commanded (politely), because we want them to come. Whatever category is applicable, every person coming to that meeting must be given reasonable notice of the meeting. In some cases a day or two (or less, in an emergency) will suffice. If the meeting is one of a regular series, then the date on which it is to take place will probably have been decided at the last meeting. If this is the case, then all we have to watch out for is any subsequent change in the date, time or location. If there has been such a change, then we must make sure that details of the change are circulated in good time.

It's usually a good idea to check that notices of meetings, or changes in arrangements for meetings are received by the people to whom they were sent. Letters and faxes can go astray. Telephone messages aren't always passed on. The more important the meeting, the more essential to make this check. If the meeting isn't important then why are we calling it? And if we've invited some people who don't need to come, we shouldn't have done. Otherwise, a quick ring round to make sure that everyone knows what is happening can save a lot of hassle later.

It is becoming increasingly unnecessary to indicate before-hand whether the meeting is to be one at which smoking is permitted or not. Most people assume nowadays that smoking isn't permitted. Indeed, more and more entire offices are becoming no-smoking zones.

Most meetings that are part of a regular series will include on their agenda minutes of the last meeting. Someone has to prepare these, and this should have been made clear to them before the last meeting, not after it. It is bad business manners to ask anyone to perform a task for which they have had an inadequate time to prepare. Minutes of last meetings should be as brief as possible, without omitting anything important. This isn't usually a problem – few people enjoy writing minutes.

The venue

Most meetings are held regularly in the same venue – a boardroom or conference room, or the office of one of the attenders. If, however, we have arranged a meeting in a room that we haven't used earlier for such a purpose, then we should check the room before the meeting takes place – preferably before we send out the notices of the meeting. It isn't a good idea to take another's word for it that 'the canteen (or wherever) is fine for meetings'. The canteen may have been fine for Barber's little *tête à tête* a couple of months ago – all he needed was a table and three chairs and a chance to gossip for an hour or two with his cronies over a cup of tea. We may need a room that is more private, more businesslike, quieter and where we shall not be interrupted by the frequent crash of tray on trolley. If so, the golden rule is to check it out first.

Any room used for a meeting (especially a meeting of any length) should be warm, well-ventilated, comfortable. Comfort doesn't have to run to the 'let's all put our feet up' level, but hard chairs do not make good meetings. Small group meetings may take place round a desk. Some meetings are conducted with people sitting in a circle. The more formal the meeting, however, the better it is to sit everyone attending at a table. This can help establish a focus on the chairperson of the meeting, who should sit either at an end of the table or in the middle position of the side of the table. It also allows people a place for any notepads they have brought with them. Tables are also useful for leaning elbows on – giving just the right amount of comfort.

If we hope that people will take notes at the meeting, then it's a good idea to supply pads and pencils at each place. We probably shan't see either again, but it does indicate clearly that we expect those attending to jot down the salient points of our brilliant summing-up at the end of the meeting.

Company rules will almost certainly dictate whether or not smoking is permissible on the premises. If smoking is banned within the office premises, then we must abide by that rule – to do otherwise may be in breach of fire regulations. If smoking is generally permitted, however, we should not assume that it is permissible at the meeting. This is especially true if outsiders have been invited. More on this in the next section of this chapter.

Duties of a chairperson
Chairing a meeting is often a thankless task, but some people manage to do it very well. It calls for patience, a sense of humour, diplomacy, honesty, an ability to arbitrate, and preparation.

Those who are experienced in chairing meetings may have their own methods of ensuring that all goes well. For the rest of us, here are a few points to bear in mind:

174

1. Before inviting anyone to a meeting, make sure that such a meeting really is necessary.
2. Decisions as to who should be invited to the meeting should be made without prejudice. Just because we cannot stand the Chief Accountant does not mean that he or she shouldn't be invited.
3. We should consult others before and after we have drawn up the agenda. Only after we have done that should the agenda be circulated.
4. Any time saved by paying sloppy attention to writing up the minutes of the last meeting will be lost once we have to deal with our mistakes and omissions during 'Matters Arising' – and we shall lose authority.
5. As early as possible on the day of the meeting, we should check the venue. If other meetings are being held in the same room before our meeting, we should especially check that the room is left in a reasonable condition. The corollary to this is, of course, that we should make sure we leave any room in which we have held a meeting in a reasonable condition.
6. We should be in good time for any meeting that we have chaired. It may seem impressive to sweep in late muttering '. . . bloody New York . . .' but, like many things that seem impressive, it's rude. Early arrival is especially important if we have invited outsiders to the meeting. We should be there to greet our guests.
7. If the meeting is likely to be a protracted one, we should arrange that refreshments are served. More on this later in the chapter.
8. The value or importance of a meeting is not measured by the length of time it takes.
9. A good meeting is one where everyone leaves feeling that their point of view has been at least adequately expressed.
10. Despite what Richard II said about 'stern alarums' being 'changed to merry meetings', the powers of a chairperson are limited. We cannot make reasonable

people out of fools, bores and manic obsessives. And yet, we have to try . . .

Running a meeting

Once everyone has been greeted and placed round the table, the chairperson should get the meeting under way at the correct time. Sometimes it's permissible to wait for an important latecomer, apologising to those present for the delay and explaining why it is necessary. In general, however, meetings should start at the appointed time. If the chairperson takes this businesslike stance from the beginning, it sets the tone for the rest of the meeting.

It may then be appropriate to introduce those present, or to ask each person to introduce themselves. The more formal the meeting, the more the responsibility for introductions lies with the chairperson. If there are outsiders at the meeting, as chairperson we should make sure that we are well briefed, and that we know the names and roles of each person present. It is bad manners to appear not to know whom we have invited.

Once the meeting is under way, the main duty of a chairperson is to make sure that it proceeds at an efficient rate, that everyone has the opportunity to voice their views, that those who probably have something important to contribute but are shy or hesitant are encouraged to speak, that nobody hijacks the meeting for their own purposes, and that slanging matches are avoided. All this has to be achieved with the right mixture of humour, firmness, impartiality and efficiency. As chairperson we may put our own views before the meeting, but this is best done after everyone else has done so. It should never appear that we are setting out to predetermine not only the way discussion should take place, but also what the result of that discussion should be. We should invite views from others. If we know that one particular person at the meeting is in the best position to begin the discussion, then it is perfectly in order for us to invite such a person to speak first.

Once discussion is underway, then we have to check that it doesn't wander from the point, that people are not simply making the same point over and over again more and more vehemently and irascibly, that both sides (should it be that sort of meeting) are having the opportunity to put their point of view. All this has to be done without it appearing that we favour one side over the other. It may be that we have to step in to keep the peace between the two sides (or more, if it's one of *those* meetings) – if so, we should do this politely but as firmly as is necessary. If a meeting that we chair degenerates into anarchic mud-slinging, the likelihood is that both sides will blame us to some degree.

An easier task is to make sure that the meeting adheres to the agenda. This isn't usually a problem because most people like to see the meeting moving towards its close as swiftly as possible, but many meetings have at least one windbag present, someone who wants to make speech after speech after speech about what was done in the old days or in Sales or in Saltoluokta. Such people persistently try to smuggle items that are not on the agenda on to the table – 'I wonder, Chair, could I presume upon the patience of the meeting at this moment in time to raise the, to me, important matter of staff toilets, lack of soap therein . . .?' They seem to believe (or pretend) that any time is ripe for AOB. Our first response may be to ask them to wait for the official AOB near the end of the meeting. Expectation that the resident windbag is going to bring up five or six such topics when the important business of the meeting has been concluded may well prompt early and hasty departures from many present. And then the meeting will become inquorate and we can all go home, leaving the windbag to pontificate to an empty room.

Once the agenda has been discussed, the chairperson should bring the meeting to an end, thanking all present (including the bore, the fool, the windbag and the manic obsessive) for attending, and, if necessary, fixing the time and place of the next meeting. It is then simply a question of ushering everyone out of the room, checking that all is in order, and rushing back to the work that has piled up while we have been having such a good time.

Attending a meeting

The devil spends much of his time tempting those of us who hate meetings. He finds such good reasons why we shouldn't go – we're busy, it's cold, we haven't anything to contribute, the last meeting was a complete waste of time, we'll miss the 3rd round replay or the Wimbledon highlights, etc. etc. If there is a valid reason why we shouldn't go to the meeting, then we should let whoever is convening the meeting know as soon as possible. If we don't have a valid excuse, then we have to grin and go.

We should prepare for the meeting by reading the minutes of the last meeting and any other relevant notes, and planning what we need to say this time. If we have been asked to bring figures or materials to the meeting, we should make sure they're ready. If we have been asked to send reports in advance of the meeting to those attending, then we should make sure they are sent in good time. Turning up with the reports at the meeting and expecting everyone to read them then and there is unacceptable.

Most meetings are simply part of the daily routine. They call for no special formalities. Sometimes, however, special meetings are called, or we are summoned to meetings that will be attended by senior members of the company or by important visitors or customers. This can raise sartorial problems. The general rule is that it's better to arrive at a meeting too formally dressed than too casually. It's always possible for a man to take off his jacket and roll up his shirt sleeves. It isn't possible suddenly to whisk off jeans and sweatshirt and replace them with a suit. For women, dressing too formally seldom presents much of a problem, though there are those men and women who react badly at such a sight – more on this in Chapter 18.

If we are likely to be late for the meeting, then the usual rules about lateness apply. We should get word to the appropriate person as quickly as possible. This is a moment when the mobile phone comes into its own. It is permissible in such circumstances to ask whoever is chairing the meeting to change the order in which items on the agenda are discussed, but we can't insist on this. The decision lies with the chairperson (and with those who aren't late for the meeting). This is one of the many reasons why it pays to be civil to him or her.

Once at the meeting, it is simply a matter of deciding when to speak and when to be silent. In formal meetings, all contributions should be channelled through the chairperson, though this may be relaxed as discussion wears on. By the time people are shouting at each other, they are unlikely to do so 'through the chair'. How well we make our points, how well we attract support for our cause, how triumphantly we carry the day will depend on a great many things – personality, preparation, timing among them. Whole books have been written on the subject of how to make friends and influence people – some have the gift, some don't. But it helps to have clear in our mind what our objectives are. Do we want to build support for further discussions at a later date? Or are we looking for victory here, now, at any cost? It's a question of whether it's better to read Machiavelli or Emily Post.

If we feel we are not being given a chance to put forward our point of view, then we may draw the chairperson's attention to this. In doing so we are making a criticism of him or her, and we should be aware of that. Justified or not, the criticism may not be well-received, so it must be made without rudeness or rancour – though we may feel obliged to make this point strongly.

Sometimes, it is helpful to have knowledge of any standing orders or constitutional guidelines that cover the conduct of meetings. If there are such rule books, the chairperson should know all about them, but he or she may have to be reminded. This is especially important if issues have to be voted on. If the constitution permits a secret ballot and we do not wish others to know how we are voting, then we may demand that voting slips are provided.

Whenever we are taking a line that is against the general feeling of the meeting, it pays to be doggedly persistent, rather than emotionally enraged. Those of us who remember the film

Shane should adopt the Alan Ladd role rather than that of Jack Palance, however tempted to do otherwise.

If, after a meeting, we do feel that we lost our temper unjustifiably or behaved in some way that was ill-mannered, then we should send a letter of apology to the chairperson as soon as possible. We should not apologise for our views, but only for the way we expressed them. Asking the chairperson to pass on our apologies to others who attended the meeting is not advisable.

Conferences

Many conferences are meetings on a grander, longer scale – weekends or weeks when meeting follows meeting follows meeting, and we end the day in the bar of the hotel holding impromptu meetings about the next day's meetings. Almost all the points raised earlier in this chapter still apply. More than ever it is important to check the venue of the meeting or conference. Few people within the company are going to thank the person who organises a conference in a hotel where the rooms are uncomfortable, the food is awful and the facilities are inadequate for the business that is to be conducted.

Most chains of hotels and independent hotels now offer 'conference facilities', but standards vary considerably as to what this should comprise. To some it's little more than a big room with a table in it. To others it means fax machines; photocopiers; easy access to many telephone lines; audio-visual aids; satellite links with business centres in Europe, North America and the rest of the world; tele-conferencing arrangements; and the whole plethora of modern business life. To avoid disappointment, or worse, such facilities should be personally checked before bookings are finalised.

For those of us who attend such conferences, we should be aware that our corporate image will be enhanced or otherwise by the way we behave in public places. If other guests at the hotel have their stay shattered by company high jinks (a little rugby in the bedroom corridors late at night; drunks plummeting to the floor in bar and restaurant; staff aggressively chatted up at every available opportunity), then we have done little for the good of our company's reputation.

In company time, on company premises, or whenever in the service of the company, we have to keep a business head on our shoulders.

CHECKLIST

1. No meeting should be held without good reason.
2. Remember that all who come to a meeting have had to leave some other task.
3. Meetings should be held in the most congenial places possible – not in broom cupboards.
4. Everyone who is entitled to be at a meeting must be invited – no matter how much we may dislike them.
5. Meetings should start and finish punctually.
6. A good chairperson is fair and efficient, not bumbling and verbose.
7. Any Other Business doesn't mean Every Other Business.
8. If we have a duty to go to a meeting, we should attend, no matter how comfortable or busy we are in our own office or the wine bar round the corner.
9. Time spent preparing for a meeting is time well spent.
10. Time spent preparing for a conference is time exceedingly well spent.

CHAPTER 18

Women in business

Your duty cannot be done unless your health is sound.
So keep constantly on your guard against any excesses.
In this new experience you may find temptations both
in wine and women. You must entirely resist both
temptations, and, while treating all women with perfect
courtesy, you should avoid any intimacy . . .

LORD KITCHENER
– Message to members of the BEF,
printed in *The Times* 19 August 1914

Feminism is the most revolutionary idea there has ever
been. Equality for women demands a change in the
human psyche more profound than anything Marx
dreamed of.

POLLY TOYNBEE – *Guardian* 19 January 1987

Apologia

I write this book as a man, and there's not a lot I can do about
that. The contents of this chapter, therefore, should be viewed
with more than average suspicion. Any suggestions from a
man as to how women should behave in the business world,
what they should wear, and how they should present themselves are very likely to be ill-focused. Women who read this
chapter will almost certainly wish to reconstruct it in the light
of their own experience. Generalisations are poor indicators at
the best of times: when they refer to matters that are in a state
of constant change, of advance and backlash, they are very
rough guides indeed, and, when they are made by someone
who cannot have experienced what he's talking about, they
may be ill-conceived.

Introduction

Many of us still perceive women in business in much the way
that they were depicted by Hollywood thirty or forty years ago
– and Hollywood's images of women aren't all that different
today. In the movies there were two sorts of business women –
secretaries and executives. Secretaries were sub-divided into
the dizzy blondes, who could barely type and talked in
squeaky voices, and the bespectacled brunettes, who were
earnest and soft-spoken and who took off their glasses in the
last reel to reveal staggering beauty and a complete absence of
business ambition. Women executives were ruthless, strident,
domineering, preying and three-quarters mad, and were
always played by Barbara Stanwyck, Bette Davis or Joan
Crawford. In the last reel they came to grief.

The fact is that women in business still present men with an
enormous dilemma – should they be treated as women or as
something else, a kind of second class male? Should a man
open the door for his female business colleague, offer to carry
her heavy pile of reports, or should he leave her to struggle
along on her own? Should he serve her coffee before the
others, or should she be serving the coffee anyway? Should he
treat her gently when admonishing her for a mistake she's
made, for fear that she might otherwise burst into tears, or
should he bawl the bitch out for having the effrontery to think
she could hold her own in a man's world?

There are no hard and fast answers to some of these
questions. Not yet. Women and men may both have some
ideas as to how they would like matters to develop, though
these ideas may sadly differ. Men worked out the rules for
men many years ago. The trouble is that they have also tried
to work out the rules for women. We are all in a wait-and-see
situation, and much dithering, suffering and arguing lie in
store. When women are equally represented in boardroom,
salesroom and conference room, we shall be nearer to resolv-
ing the dilemmas. The problem at the moment is that men
think the problem is women, and women think the problem is
men.

Fair play or fair sex?

There are still a few men around who claim there is nothing wrong in patting a woman's backside, stroking her arm or nuzzling up to her at work, but only a fool would believe that such behaviour is permissible. There are many more men around who believe that there is nothing wrong in calling a woman 'dear', 'love', 'beautiful', 'darling', etc. Some women do not mind, but a great many do, so such patronising familiarity should be avoided. If the excuse offered for such ludicrous behaviour is that 'I was only being friendly', then the man responsible should consider the reaction if he called a male colleague 'handsome' or 'muscles', just because he was trying to be friendly.

All this is now more than a matter of good and bad manners. More and more legislation covers behaviour at work, and however much some may sneer at the notion of political correctness, and however much some may appear to be pushing it to ridiculous extremes, the days of carefree sexual harassment at work are almost over. Sexual harassment is perforce at least a more furtive occupation than it was a generation ago.

For some people, however, the subtleties of what constitutes sexual harassment are bewildering. There are plenty of men who see nothing wrong in putting their arm round a female colleague who is distressed, in a protective and comforting way. Indeed, they do not see what else they could reasonably do – for to leave the woman to her tears seems cruel and heartless. Many women might also see no harm in such an action, but it is dangerous to make assumptions.

I have a friend in California whom I shall call Potter. Potter is a soft-spoken middle-aged guy, happily married and pleasantly friendly to one and all. He taught art in a women's prison. In California, business etiquette is very strictly defined when it comes to the behaviour of men towards women. Potter had already been in trouble for one or two ill-judged remarks to female colleagues and had been sent on a consciousness raising course to improve his attitude. One day he

185

entered an office at work and came across a female colleague. She was wearing a smart jacket, and beneath it what Potter called 'one of those kinda see-through blouses'. He's not sure how long he gazed at her before he was aware that she noticed what he was doing. He then said: 'Nice jacket'. The woman accused him of sexual harassment. He was summoned before a tribunal and lost his job, to his mind because he uttered those two words. Those who have seen David Mamet's play *Oleanna* may know how shattering can be the reverberations of an ill-judged remark or action such as this. The more Potter talked about his misfortune, the more it became clear that those two words were merely the tip of an iceberg. He meant no harm, but he did have a problem in his attitude to some women colleagues. What he regarded as friendliness caused offence and broke the rules.

The moral of Potter's story may be simply that men and women who work together must be ever on their guard. In an article entitled 'And then she kissed me . . .' in the *Observer* (23 January 1994), Rosalind Crawford wrote: 'The prevailing "backlash" view in America is that all claims of sexual harassment against men come either from female harassers or from harridans wielding the weapons of political correctness in their vendettas against men.' But it isn't a question of who is to blame – is the woman being over-sensitive, or is the man being under-sensitive? It's a question of how and when do we all find the solution to the problem of relating to the opposite sex with no more problems than we have in relating to our own. Potter's sorry story took place in California, and there are those who believe that it couldn't take place in Britain. I think they're wrong.

A few basics
Squinting through the mists of controversy, we may discern one or two guiding beacons, applicable to men and women:

1. Colleagues are colleagues and should be treated as individuals, not as representatives of their gender.

2. If men or women ask us to hold the door open or carry something for them, we need a good reason not to oblige – a request for help should not be the prelude to a row about equality. And, to use the language of dear old Lord Kitchener, courtesy should not be seen as the first step on the path to intimacy.
3. No one should barge through a door first letting it slam in the faces of those following.
4. On the other hand, opening a door for someone else in a way that hints they are incapable of looking after themselves is creepy behaviour.
5. Women should not be expected to do more than a fair share of making or fetching coffee, or doing the washing-up.
6. On the other hand, women should not rush to do the washing-up and clearing away as though their male business colleagues had just completed a twelve hour shift at the pit face.
7. At meetings and conferences, women should not have to make extra efforts in order to make their contributions.
8. On the other hand, men running meetings shouldn't condescendingly invite contributions from women colleagues.
9. No one should be subjected to remarks laced with sexual innuendo or sexual disparagement.
10. The concepts that men can't help what they do, and women can't help what they do, should be abandoned.

It isn't always easy to keep in mind that what is needed here is a reciprocal solution to a reciprocal problem. Because the business world is still dominated by men, progress towards a fairer system is seen mainly in terms of what needs to be done by and for women. The focus is on how men should treat their women colleagues, rather than *vice versa*. One day we may discover that what matters most is how we all treat each other.

Then it will be acceptable for some men to loathe working with some women, and some women to loathe working with some men, and some men to like working with some women, and some women to like working with some men. Until this wonderful day is reached, perhaps we had better all be on our guard.

Dressing for business

Men have an enormous advantage over women when it comes to dressing for business. In the first place, the range of clothes available to men, in colour and style and material, is extremely limited, and in the second place, no one really seems to care what men wear. A suit is a suit is a suit. If a man turns up for a meeting in a crumpled, shiny, ill-fitting suit, few people are surprised. We do not expect men to be discerning or imaginative in the clothes they buy. We do not judge them by the clothes they wear, though there are signs that men who have managed to make the sartorial quantum leap beyond Marks and Spencer's gain extra points. We still assume that they haven't chosen their own outfits, but have been guided by a woman.

It's very different for women, who do have a choice. Women in business are very much judged by what they wear, which is perhaps why it appears that women are increasingly 'playing it safe' – wearing female equivalents of menswear, trouser suits or suits with skirts, tailored in masculine styles and made out of material that is indistinguishable from that worn by men. This may be only a compromise solution to the problem of what to wear for business, but it works at the moment. Few eyebrows are raised at such outfits. The impression given is business-like, smart, practical. Because women are not only judged by what they wear, but also by how well they wear it, other problems arise. The fattest man in the world isn't mocked or criticised for wearing trousers – many women are. A man who wears trousers that are a little short in the leg may cause a snigger or two, but, once business discussions get under way, all will be forgotten. A woman who wears a skirt that is a little short may find that this has a profound and destructive influence on her working life. A man who shaves badly is to be pitied. A woman who applies make-up badly is to be scorned. A man who wears what every other man in the room is wearing is entitled to feel at ease. A woman who wears what one other woman in the room is wearing should feel ashamed of herself.

At the risk of rushing in where males should fear to tread, here are a few points to consider:

1. The cut and quality of women's clothes are more often noticed than those of men.
2. The more extrovert, individual, or exciting a woman's clothes, the less she will be judged for her business skill by most men and many women.
3. Opinions may vary as to whether the above is a good or bad thing.
4. A woman who wears too much jewellery during the working day may seem to be flaunting her wealth or her luck or her connections, and will make few friends and influence few people the right way.
5. Applying make-up in public still attracts a lot of criticism.
6. Comfortable shoes are better than smart shoes for working purposes. Shoes that are both smart and comfortable are in a class of their own.
7. Don't wear unprotected smart clothes to do the washing-up in the office. Better to get some shabby man to do it.
8. A man may spend an entire weekend at a business conference in one set of clothes. A woman will be expected to wear at least four different outfits.
9. At receptions, dinner dances, office parties and business trips to Henley, Lords, Wimbledon or Glyndebourne, women are expected to dress as women by most men and many women.
10. A hole in a man's sock is a sign that he cares too much

about his work: a ladder in a woman's tights is a sign
that she doesn't care enough.

Many of the old myths about women's clothes are still given
some credence, especially those that are derogatory or
demean women. Very high heels and ankle bracelets denote a
tart. Too much make-up is 'cheap'. Low necklines are the
mark of a fast woman. Women who wear severely cut trouser
suits and have their hair cut short are gay. Women who tie
their hair in a bun and wear spectacles should take their
glasses off and let their hair down. A tight sweater signifies
loose morals. Women who wear brightly coloured clothes are
trying to attract men. 'There is invariably something odd
about women who wear ankle socks'. The list is long and
depressing, but, for the moment at least, women may have to
consider it as they dress for another day's work.

Women in charge
The same duality of standards between men and women
applies at higher levels in the business world. It is generally
accepted that a man may shout to stress his authority, but
women are not entitled to 'screech' – the very words we use
reveal the unfairness of the situation. Men may be 'aggressive'
– women are allowed to be only 'assertive'. A man who speaks
ill of his rivals or colleagues behind their backs is 'ambitious' –
a woman who does the same is 'bitchy'. A man who is seldom
satisfied with the work of his minions is 'tough' – a woman
who is similarly hard to please is 'shrewish'. On the other
hand, when a woman seems to be getting her way by female
strategies, this isn't fair either. The business world is a
minefield for women at the best of times, and the further they
advance, the more mines have been strewn in their paths.

Men call the shots, make the running, lay down the rules.
The best approach for a woman is to ignore gender differentia-
tions and to act in a way that seems polite and reasonable. If a
man wants to open a door, fine. If a man doesn't want to open
a door, fine. If a senior woman is taking a male colleague,

client or customer out to lunch, then she should play the role of host – she decides where to eat, what wine to drink, offers advice as to what to order based on her own experience of the restaurant. Similarly, if a woman is chairing a meeting, she decides what is to go on the agenda, when discussion on any one point has been sufficient, when someone should be encouraged to make their contribution. If a junior colleague (male or female) has been guilty of some negligence or omission or transgression, the woman in authority administers the admonishment or dismisses the culprit. Each case has to be decided on its merits, each scenario may need a different script. But in running her office or department in this way, a woman is not only doing the right thing, she is pointing the way for men to follow.

Sadly, however, there are occasions when women have to behave in an artificially businesslike way. The business woman travelling alone has far less freedom to relax than a man. This isn't so much a matter of etiquette as survival. A woman driving on her own needs a mobile phone and membership of one of the breakdown agencies. If her car does break down, she should telephone for assistance, stay in her car and lock the doors. She should decline offers of help from passing male motorists. If a woman is staying on her own at a hotel, she should suggest by her clothes and attitude that she is on strictly a business visit. It may be that she has to wear business clothes at all times and that she has to carry a briefcase and sheaves of paper even into the hotel dining room in the evening. She should take care where and how she sits in bar and restaurant, avoiding appearing 'accessible'. If a woman is approached by a man while on her own, she should be frigidly polite in asking the man to leave her alone. If he doesn't, then the woman should call a member of the hotel staff and ask them to deal with the problem. And, at all times, a woman has to be on her guard against the sad fact that many men mistake friendliness for flirtation, laughter for lust, and enjoyment for encouragement.

PART TWO
Business Etiquette Abroad

CHAPTER 19

European business etiquette

We were challenged with a choice between the American
system of rugged individualism and a European philosophy of diametrically opposed doctrines – doctrines of
paternalism and state socialism.

HERBERT HOOVER
– Speech in New York City, October 1928

General introduction

Historically, Europe has experienced more wars than any
other continent. However united or peaceful it may seem now
(*pace* Yugoslavia), for centuries the Dutch fought the Spanish
and the British, the Germans fought the French, the Italians
fought each other, and the British fought everybody. Under
the hopefully ever-thickening veneer of civilisation, there may
well be atavistic forces rumbling away like grumbling appen-
dixes under the skin. Old wounds take a long time to heal
completely, but part of the healing process is to manifest
respect for the culture and traditions of others.

One of the best ways of doing this is to make some attempt
to learn the language of a country with which we are dealing.
Millions of Danes and Dutch speak excellent English. Luxem-
bourg is a truly multi-lingual society. The French, we suspect,
are capable of understanding and speaking English perfectly
well but stubbornly refuse to do so. But English is not the only
language in the world – it isn't even the only language in
Britain – and time taken to learn how to say 'good morning',
'please' and 'thank you' in the tongue of the people we are
visiting is time well spent.

It is worth remembering that many European countries
have more than one 'native' language (Catalan in Spain;

195

Flemish as well as French in Belgium; dialect versions of Italian – particularly in Tuscany). It is also important to be aware of strong local or regional feelings in Europe. We all know (or should know) that the Scots and the Welsh resent being lumped together with the English; but, where relevant, we should also be aware, for example, that the Basques of both south-west France and north-east Spain are a proud and independent people, many of them at professional and business level.

It is pushing optimism too far to expect speculative letters or publicity handouts or sales brochures written in English to end up anywhere other than the waste paper basket, unread. On the other hand, amateur translations into Italian or Portuguese or whatever will always be regarded with scorn and laughter. If we can't write a reasonable letter, the thinking will go, what on earth are our products like? Even those who speak and write good English themselves take note of British business people who have the courtesy and intelligence to use their own languages – but best to have such translations made, or at least checked, by an expert.

There is no substitute for visiting potential markets before committing ourselves to a pitch. Indeed, frequent visiting is much recommended. Europe isn't a huge continent, as continents go, but it pays to show that we are accessible, and prepared to travel regularly.

FRANCE

Background
France was one of the earliest nation states of Europe. Louis XIV, and others, always considered that God had fashioned France's natural borders – the Pyrenees, the Alps, the Mediterranean, the Rhine, the Atlantic and the Channel. It has also had one of the most effective centralised governments, since the time of Napoleon Bonaparte. The French may hurl rage and abuse at their governments, but they look to them to

manage the economy, protect and promote industry, and maintain French cultural supremacy. They will accept criticism of their government (after all they repeatedly demonstrate against it by blockading cities with tractors, burning vast piles of old tyres and hurling stones at government lackeys – such as the police), but they take exception to criticisms of the French way of life, French culture, and over-all Frenchness.

Bosses and workers

Qualifications, education and training are enormously respected in France. If a person has formal qualifications for a job, then he or she is viewed as an expert and his or her pronouncements are far less likely to be questioned than those of a similar expert in Britain. In France qualifications are often seen as more important than experience.

Outsiders need to appreciate that, although France has proportionately far lower trade union membership among its workers than most European countries, where unions do exist and are strong, they are highly politicised. Far more attention in France is paid to workers on the lower rungs of a company ladder. Reports on performance by managers will include appraisals by junior staff. There is more consultation with workers on the part of management. It doesn't do to assume, therefore, that work patterns, the role of managers and the whole company hierarchy follow British patterns.

Executives of companies are subject to many more legally imposed duties and restrictions than their British counterparts. It is wrong, therefore, to assume that French heads of companies are being deliberately obstructive if they say they are unable to meet certain demands or deadlines. There may well be a valid legal reason for their inability to oblige. This is so despite the highly paternalistic structure of a large number of French businesses, many of which seek to create what amounts to a family sense of loyalty and shared experience.

Business practice

Most French businesses are highly structured. They contain many layers of middle management. There is a chain of command that rigidly preserves the differentials between each grade or rank in the company hierarchy. Outsiders may have to anticipate delays in communication between departments and layers of management – far more than in the United States or Britain. This has to be respected. It is not a good idea to adopt a 'well you people may have your funny old way of doing business but I think it's best if we all muck in together' approach.

French industry is led from the top. Just as the President of the republic may have a vision of the future of France, so the Chief Executive (le President Directeur General) may well have a vision of the future of his or her company. This means that it can prove extremely difficult to persuade a French company to change its policy, its direction, its specifications, its requirements and procedures. To do so might well mean someone at the top having to admit that he or she was wrong. But the PDG may have a greater understanding of the factory floor working procedures of the company than his or her counterpart in Britain. The French admire workshop knowledge and expect representatives of foreign companies to have the same degree of technical expertise that they have.

The French do not like being surrounded by too many targets or deadlines. Failure to reach such goals would be taken personally, or at least attributed to the person in charge. This means that it may appear that the French distrust teamwork and the whole concept of a team, feeling that, once they are part of a team, their perceived success or lack of it is inextricably linked to the performance of others. Again, the model to bear in mind is that of a family – squabbling siblings rather than co-operating colleagues.

Formality in France

The French love formality. Their greetings are highly formal, whether a handshake or a deft kiss on the cheek.

French colleagues working in the same office will shake each others' hands every day of the working year when they meet in the morning, and perhaps once more when they part in the evening. The average French person takes a dim view of those who forget names or the time and place of previous meetings. It is most important for outsiders to commit to memory the names and titles of any French business associate or client to whom they are introduced. There is still an air of formality about the daily greetings of colleagues who have worked together for years: 'Bonjour, Monsieur (or Madame) Ducroix' rather than 'Bonjour, Henri (or Bernadette)'. This is especially true when the greeting is made in front of third parties. The French like the same apparent solemnity from their visitors.

This sense of formality is carried into their business meetings. Every meeting in France, whether to consider the allocation of parking spaces in the company car park or the overthrow of the government, has a rigid agenda. The French come well-prepared and well-briefed to such meetings and expect others to do the same. Criticism of a business plan or proposal tends to be taken personally. Since they see everyone attending the meeting as a personal rival, they are unlikely to indulge in sessions of shared brain-storming or problem-solving. Meetings, like companies themselves, are led from the top, and it is courting disaster to go against the decisions or advice of the chairperson.

Visitors to France should expect to be presented at first with what appears to be a high degree of professional frigidity. This should not be questioned, though it may later emerge that there is a second, semi-secret, informal way of doing business.

Dress
The French do not have the extremes of dress that are to be found in British working life. They seldom wear dark, three piece suits and are unlikely to be found in jeans and

sweatshirt. They dress with casual formality – jacket and trousers for men, trouser suits or smart blouse and skirt for women. It is the quality rather than the *genre* of dress that matters to them. Outsiders should not run the risk of dressing too informally for business in France. Over-dressing, however, is not only excused, it is frequently admired.

Social occasions
Entertaining a friend, colleague or visitor is far more likely to take place in a restaurant or bar than in the host's own home. The French are a public people, made for special occasions, and in many cases they are more 'at home' in a cafe than in their own *sejours*. They are proud of their knowledge of local restaurants and local food and wine, and it would be considered the height of bad manners to pretend, as an outsider, that we knew better than they which wine to drink with which cheese.

Punctuality
Despite their strong belief in protocol, manners and the proprieties of life, the French can be dreadful time-keepers. They are often late for appointments, meetings, and interviews. There is a special French concept of time, it would appear, so that being 'on time' means 'being within fifteen minutes of the appointed hour'. It is not a good idea to follow French practice here, for they expect foreigners to be punctual.

Humour
Jokes are much rarer in France than they are in Britain – they go for quality rather than quantity. Jokes should be intellectually witty as well as funny, apposite, timely and well delivered. Personal remarks, no matter how wittily delivered or how jokingly intended, are always likely to be regarded with effrontery by the French.

BELGIUM

Background

Belgium has existed as an independent state since 1830. Formerly, it was the Catholic region of what were known as the Southern Netherlands. Although it is one country, Belgium is composed of two very separate parts: Flanders, in the agricultural north, and Wallonia, in the industrial south. In Flanders most people speak Flemish. In Wallonia, most people speak French. It is reckoned that most of the inhabitants of Belgium see themselves as Walloons or Flemings first, Europeans second, and Belgians third. Certainly Flanders owes a great deal to the European Community, having been the poor relation of its neighbour for the first 120 years of Belgium's existence.

This background is important. Visitors to Belgium should see themselves as dealing with either Walloons or Flemings, and should at least study and try to use the relevant language. It is unrealistic to expect either Flemings or Walloons to wax lyrical about each other, though, obviously, no good long-term process is served by running either side down. The split between the two is deep and appears permanent. Dual ministries have been created to cover almost every aspect of government. Better, therefore, to think of Belgium as two nations rather than one.

Whether a company is Flemish or Walloon is indicated by the initials that follow the name of the company in its registered title. Flemish companies are denoted by either NA (*Naamloze Vennootschnapp* – public company) or BVBA (*Beslote Vennootschnapp met Beperkte Aansprakelijkheid* – private company). Walloon companies are denoted by SA or SPRL, corresponding to the French titles (*Société Anonyme* or *Société Privée a Responsabilité Limitée*).

Brussels is something of an oddity, a French-speaking city in the middle of Flanders, with more of a European than a Belgian identity. English is accepted as a business language more in Brussels than in any other part of Belgium. In fact,

201

25% of the city's population is made up of foreigners, almost all of them working for the European Community in one capacity or another.

Bosses and workers

Belgium has always been a nation that relied heavily on trade. Antwerp is the third largest port in the world. Industry is less state-owned, state-controlled or state-influenced than in France. Trade union membership is higher than in France. There is, however, a similarly progressive attitude towards worker participation in management. Every company with more than 100 employees has to establish a works council composed of equal numbers of representatives from management and workers.

Business practice

The Belgians (both the Flemish and, to a lesser extent, the Walloons) do not share the French preoccupation with formality and hierarchy within the workplace, nor the enormous sense of national pride. They have a very different historical perspective – there is no sense that God created Belgium. Except when threatened by invading armies, they have always tended to believe in negotiation and compromise, in politics and in business. Neither do they share the French enthusiasm for the new, the daring, the challenging – whatever the cost.

Rank and status within the company is far less important among the Belgians than the French. Few Belgian bosses adopt the paternalistic approach of many of their French counterparts. The Walloons, however, are nearer to the French in their business methods than the Flemings. They like their companies to be structured, with a clear hierarchy of personnel. They are diligent in their work and expect others to be the same. Like the Flemings, they may lack French flair, but make up for this in their application to and concentration on their work. It is this, sadly, that makes all Belgians the butt of so many French jokes.

Formality
The Walloons are as formal as the French, the Flemings are even more formal. Decades may pass before first names are used in Flanders, and it is essential for outsiders to stick to 'Mejneer' or 'Mevrouw' followed by the family name in conversation. In Wallonia, it is similarly best to stick to 'Monsieur' or 'Madame', as in France.

Social occasions
The Belgians all enjoy good food, though they do not go to the French lengths of making eating and drinking appear almost the only reasons for living. It is courteous to drink and commend the excellent Belgian beer, rather than German or French wine, while in Belgium, and it's worth remembering that the Belgians make the best pastries and patisseries and perhaps the best chocolate in the world. Most social gatherings are likely to be formal occasions, and it is best for outsiders to observe quietly how the meal or the evening is progressing and unfolding before launching into any riotous imported behaviour.

Humour
The Belgians are more likely to see obsessive preoccupation with inappropriate or misplaced humour as eccentric rather than rude. In both Flanders and Wallonia, it is better to avoid making jokes merely for the sake of it. What is intended to lighten the atmosphere may have the opposite effect. If we cannot stop our waggish selves being the life and soul of every meeting, we should do business in Wallonia rather than Flanders.

Although the French publish entire books of jokes against the Belgians, the Flemings and the Walloons are forgiving people, and it is said that they tell much better anti-Belgian jokes than outsiders do. The old joke about there being so few famous Belgians has worn very thin and certainly doesn't travel well to Belgium itself.

GERMANY

Background

Although much of present day Germany was part of the Holy Roman Empire in medieval times, the existence of a unified German state is relatively new. It took some brilliant diplomacy and two swiftly and efficiently executed wars in the second half of the 19th century to produce a German nation from the earlier kingdoms and princedoms and electorates of Brandenburg, Prussia, Bavaria, Saxony, etc.

For the first fifty years or so, up to 1918, Germany was a monarchy, ruled by the Kaisers. Since then Germany has gone through many political changes, many of which it is best not to dwell on. It also helps to remember the advice of Basil Fawlty, 'Don't mention the war'. Today, Germany is again united, with a democratic government and an economy which is still envied by many other nations.

Like Britain, Germany has traditionally had a north-south divide, but on a religious basis, the north being predominantly Protestant, the south predominantly Catholic. There was also, of course, an east-west divide after the Second World War until the Berlin Wall was demolished in 1992. The east-west divide is now a thing of the past, but it is important to remember that for more than a generation the economic, political and, to a lesser extent, the social experiences of east and west Germans were very dissimilar.

Partly as a result of this, and partly as a result of earlier history, Germany is less centralised in economic and administrative terms than, say, France or Britain. Berlin is the traditional capital of Germany, but Bonn is the centre of government. Hamburg has always been the most important German port and the centre for trade. The Ruhr has been the heart of Germany's massive industrial output. Frankfurt is the banking capital of Germany. This geographical spread of interests is less inconvenient than it may appear, for Germany has probably the best road and rail system in Europe.

Prejudice

The first essential before having any contact with the German business world is to rid our minds of all the old stereotypical images with which we have been bombarded in films, comic books, comedy routines and tabloid newspapers. The Germans are not fat, ruthless, warmongering people devoid of a sense of humour. No European nation holds a monopoly of intolerance, xenophobia or aggressiveness – indeed, it is impossible even to work out in which order the nations of Europe should be placed for any quality, positive or negative. But the German people have had an ill-deserved bad press in Britain for too long, and we need to be on our guard against the effects of that.

Bosses and workers

Although German industry and commerce boasts some great names (Krupps, Mercedes, Volkswagen *et al*), the average German company is relatively small in size. Though not as paternalistic in outlook and control as the French, many German firms are run more along the lines of a family than are their British counterparts. This manifests itself in two ways: German management usually show considerable concern for the welfare of their workers, but daddy knows best and management recruits often feel excluded from the day-to-day decision making process of the company for which they work. Those in charge of German businesses like to make long-term plans for the future of their company and do not expect opposition to their plans from government, banks or their own middle managers.

In terms of numbers, Germany is less unionised than Britain, but more unionised than France. By law, any company employing more than five workers must establish a works council if this is the wish of the employees. This council is composed solely of employees and must be consulted regularly by management. The council has little outright power, but the expectation is that its views will be carefully considered by management. This has led in general to a smooth-running partnership between employer and employee in most German businesses. Workers expect to be consulted on most decisions that affect their futures – security of employment, working conditions, recruitment and redundancies, pay, holidays, etc. We may have been led to believe that Britain has more strikes than Germany – in fact the reverse is true. But strikes in Germany tend to be short-lived affairs, often ending with surprisingly little acrimony on either side. They are seen as the signal that a period of careful and intense negotiation is needed, rather than as a declaration of industrial war.

Business practice

German business practice is usually carefully structured and well-ordered. Method and routine and hard work are preferred to pragmatism and the inspirational approach. Anyone dealing with a German company should stick to the timetable agreed and the terms of the contract as closely as possible. To fail to meet delivery dates, to be late for meetings, to say one thing and do another, is to build up mistrust rapidly and gain a lasting reputation for unreliability. Even if something goes wrong unexpectedly, or simply through bad luck, the unhappy experience that results will produce uncomfortable feelings that could well terminate the business relationship. It is always best, therefore, in the words of Macbeth, to 'make assurance double sure'. It is bad practice, and bad manners in the eyes of many Germans, to approach business with any appearance of lightheartedness, flippancy or any attitude that suggests less than 100% commitment. Being able to think quickly on the feet is no substitute for methodical planning. Iron, rather than mercury, is the favoured mineral.

German senior management seldom invite ideas from middle management or outsiders. To attempt to force our way, as outsiders, into internal discussions would be seen as rude, and possibly dangerous or threatening. The Germans prefer to invite opinions rather than have them come thudding in through the door unheralded and unsolicited. They share with the French a respect for the authority of those in responsible positions, but place perhaps more emphasis on experience and track-record than on technical or academic qualifications. Like the French, they expect management to have some first-hand experience of factory floor practice. Outsiders who appear to view with revulsion the notion of rolling up their sleeves and getting their hands dirty are regarded with contempt. At all times outsiders should avoid losing their tempers when conducting business in Germany. Anger is a sign of weakness, not strength. Forcefulness is sometimes interpreted as bluster.

Agreements, contracts, decisions and almost all business plans should, ultimately, be in writing. Germans are happier than the French with the notion of teamwork, but the team usually has to be formally constituted. Groups established on an *ad hoc* basis may be distrusted.

Social arrangements

The German practice when a meeting has been arranged is to provide refreshments before the meeting begins, rather than during the meeting itself. It is considered bad manners to call someone at home on a business matter unless it is of extreme urgency (which in itself may subsequently be seen as an indication of bad planning and preparation). The same is true of interruptions to holidays or times with the family. The Germans work hard, and feel that they have earned their time off. There is none of the American belief that 'they' own as much of your time as 'they' want. The Germans are in many ways a traditional people, and it is still harder for women to work their way to senior positions in business companies in Germany than in most other European countries.

Socially and privately, the Germans are markedly polite and tidy, but British people may find their preparedness to point out the mistakes and *faux pas* of others disconcerting. It can take a long time to establish first name relationships. In general, the correct way to address a German associate is as 'Herr' or 'Frau' (not 'Fraulein'), followed by the family name.

Titles (Doctor, etc.) should always be used. Before making contact, therefore, we need to do our homework and study the personnel details on business cards or company literature. Even more so than in France, the plural form of 'you' should be used at all times – *Sie*, not *Du*. Greetings and farewells are formal and regular, taking place every morning and afternoon. One stereotypical adjective may remain with us – the Germans are punctual.

Dress

Although the British business suit is not *de rigueur* in Germany, semi-formal dress is. Unlike the French, German men (and women) tend to keep their jackets on throughout the working day (unless they are alone). Work is taken seriously, and casual clothes are seen as a mark of lack of application to the task in hand. It is better to risk over-dressing in Germany than to risk being too informal.

Humour

The Germans do have a sense of humour, though they may use it more sparingly and more selectively than the British. Jocularity for jocularity's sake is unlikely to meet with approval. Work is taken seriously and not until the atmosphere is extremely relaxed and jokes have already been made should we launch into our blisteringly funny routine. One good joke will get a far better reception than any routine.

The exception to this rule is when the Germans indulge in what is known as *Fastnacht* or Carnival. At such times almost anything goes – including red noses and funny costumes.

ITALY

Background

After centuries of separation into independent kingdoms, provinces of the Austrian and French empires and Papal States, Italians fought to establish a unified country between

1861 and 1870. Like Germany, the new Italy looked for colonies in Africa and even hoped for territorial gains in Europe. As in Germany, expansionist ideas under a 20th century dictator led to political, economic and social disaster. Since 1945, despite a reputation for frequent changes of government, Italy has proved a stable democracy, one of the senior partners in the European Community. Culturally, the Italians have a history and tradition second to none.

Bosses and workers

Italy is a land of regular political referenda on important issues, which gives many Italians a taste for being consulted about important decisions. Most of them approve of state intervention in the economy and of government control of key industries and services. But there are many famous names in Italian private industry (Fiat and Olivetti perhaps foremost among them), and there is a paternalistic approach to running these private companies similar to that found in Germany. This is especially true of the industrial north of the country, where the majority of firms are small to medium size and still favour old-fashioned business methods. This may not lead to the greatest possible efficiency, but on the whole it helps to improve relationships between employers and employees, with little labour or union opposition. Every firm employing more than fifteen workers has to set up a works committee, similar to those established in Germany, but with less support and less trust from both employers and employees.

With 40% of the workforce members of trade unions, Italy is about as unionised as Germany. Unlike unions in France or Britain, unions are not craft or occupation based, but are aligned together under the banners of the main political parties. There are Christian Democrat unions, Communist unions, and so on. Many of the workers who do not belong to unions have little protection against low wages or exploitation, and confrontation between workers and bosses in these cases is common in Italy.

Business practice

The Italians present a more happy-go-lucky approach to business than most of their rivals. They have the French fondness of flair, and are often eager to cut corners. Unlike the Germans, the Italians believe wholeheartedly in pragmatism, which they sometimes carry to absurd lengths. It is thus difficult to keep fully abreast of what is happening in a business transaction with an Italian firm. There can be an air of theatricality about every operation. The cast may change, the dialogue may change, the play itself may change. Outsiders just have to do the best they can to keep up with these changes, and be ready for daily changes of plans.

This state of affairs is partly caused by the Italian system of management, which admits a high degree of personal initiative in business matters. The head of a firm will issue his or her (usually his) instructions, but these will be modified, extended, revised, etc. by several middle managers as the project proceeds. In all this, Italian practice differs greatly from that of the Germans. Italians are very like the Germans in their admiration for those in management who have technical skills, and their disdain for those who have purely administrative skills.

Lack of formality

Meetings in Italy are far less formal than those in France or Germany. Attempts to impose order and method (or an agenda) will not be met with disapproval, however. The Italians have long been extremely gracious in their preparedness and ability to accommodate the eccentricities of foreigners. It is wise not to expect such attempts to meet with any success.

The same informality applies to deals and agreements. The Italians tend to rely more on the spoken word than the Germans. Eventually it may be necessary to agree every tiny clause and put it in writing, but many deals are struck in Italy without resort to pen, paper, word processor or fax machine. At times, this informality and corner cutting can border on what appears to be sharp practice.

It is tempting to say that it doesn't so much matter what we do in Italy as how well we do it. Lateness (which can be considered a grave sin) can be turned into a positive advantage if there is a good reason for it, and the apology is expressed with style and charm. Those of us who do not possess sufficient charm or theatrical ability would do better not to be late.

Social arrangements

Italians are fond of social occasions, at which they are often to be seen to their best advantage. They are family people, and outsiders can expect to be invited into an Italian home to meet several generations, to be extremely well fed and to be graciously entertained. They are proud of their culture, and tend not to have the eclectic approach of the British in terms of food, fashion and fun. Italy is not a country where Indian, Chinese, Thai and Japanese restaurants are to be found in every town. Too much of life centres around Italy for that to happen.

However, more than most Europeans, Italians are interested in the manners and culture of others. Not to do in Rome as the Romans do will not be taken as rude. It may seem a curious way to behave, but it won't be seen as an inappropriate way to behave. Nevertheless, it helps to have some understanding of Italian etiquette. As in France and Germany, initial greetings should be formal. It's best to address Italian associates as 'Signor' or 'Signora' (rather than 'Signorina', even for young women), followed by the family name. There is not the same punctilious approach to titles (Doctor, etc.), but it pays to use them where appropriate. Better to show too much respect in Italy, rather than not enough – the Italians appreciate that.

Work should be left at the office. The Italians do not like to talk shop at home or when out at a restaurant in the evening. The work ethic may be more strictly applied in the north, but it is best not to call an Italian on a business matter outside working hours unless there is a very good reason to do so.

Modesty is not prized by the Italians, and pride is seen as a fine thing. They admire those who want to 'sell' themselves forcefully, especially if the selling is done with style.

Humour
Italians like fun. They laugh at the incongruous and the ridiculous. They are less fond of jokes which are crowbarred into the conversation. Italy is not the place to preface some irrelevant quip with 'Did you hear the one about . . .?' At all costs, we should avoid poking fun at the Italians themselves when they are being serious and their dignity is at stake.

THE NETHERLANDS

Background
The Dutch fought long and hard against enormous odds to gain their independence in the 16th and 17th centuries. Their revolt against Spanish rule from 1566 to 1648 was the longest lasting rebellion in modern European history. Within four years of obtaining their independence, they were attacked by the English, and they spent thirty-eight of the first sixty-five years of their independence having to fight either England or France or both.

With such a tough infancy, it is hardly surprising that the Netherlands has proved to be one of the most resilient countries of all time. Apart from wars against avaricious neighbours, the Dutch have had to fight the sea to build and preserve almost a quarter of the land mass of their country. They have won and lost an overseas empire and have survived invasion and blockade during the course of their relatively short history.

The country is composed of several regions or provinces (Friesland, Holland, Brabant, Gelderland, etc.); those in the south tending to be Catholic, those in the north Protestant. The country is small and crowded. It has an area of 36,000 square kilometres (about one seventh of the size of Britain), and a population of about 14 million. Rotterdam is the busiest port in Europe and one of the busiest in the world. Amsterdam is the industrial capital of the country. The Hague is the centre of government. Few countries have better transport systems, whether road, rail, air or water.

Depending on our own point of view, the Dutch are either admired for or condemned for having a remarkably progressive and tolerant view of what some see as the plagues of the 20th century – sex and drugs. Their position on rock and roll is less clear.

Bosses and workers

The Dutch have always been a great trading and business people, with some of the greatest names in modern industrialism (Philips, Shell and Unilever). There are also many small companies in the Netherlands, but the giants employ nearly a quarter of the workforce between them. The Dutch believe in private enterprise, though they also believe in good welfare provision. Proportionally, the Dutch are about as unionised as the Germans or the Italians, with a less confrontational approach to employer-employee relations than has bedevilled British industry.

Any company employing more than thirty-five workers has to set up a works council, and even those firms small enough to fall outside this requirement must consult with their workforce at least twice a year on important matters relating to employment. Worker participation at board level has existed for some time in the Netherlands, and is more highly respected than in Italy.

Business practice

The Dutch manage to combine aspects of the best business practice of their neighbours, the French and the Germans. They have the German application and commitment to hard, methodical work and sound research. At the same time they have some of the French flair and imagination.

Senior managers are expected to understand and, preferably, have some experience of all aspects of production within the company they work for. The Dutch tend to stay in one company for much of their working life. There is some distrust of and resistance to the notion of bringing in senior managers from outside the company, but the Dutch business world is not an open society in terms of ease of promotion from factory floor to boardroom. Workers and managers form two distinct classes.

The Dutch adopt a formal approach to much of the day-to-day routine of running a company. Meetings have set agendas and everyone attending a meeting will be expected to make a contribution. The Dutch prefer opinions, even dissenting ones, to be voiced openly – there is no place for the 'well, I did wonder at the time . . .' approach. They are suspicious of the man or woman who flaunts expertise or tries to impress as a high-flyer. Success (and failure) are corporate, cooperative phenomena. Outsiders are admired for hard work and humility rather than charisma and conceit. Women are less likely to reach managerial positions in the Netherlands than in Britain, France or the United States.

Social arrangements
Because almost every Dutch man and woman speaks such excellent English, there is a tendency for outsiders to drop their guard when in the Netherlands and assume that codes of manners and norms of behaviour are much the same as in Britain. Although the Dutch are friendly and informal, they do, however, stick to their own rules of etiquette. First names are used far more widely and far earlier in a relationship than in Germany or France, but initially it is considered correct to use 'Mijnheer' or 'Mevrouw' (as in Belgium) followed by the family name. Titles are sometimes used, but no points will be lost if these are accidentally omitted.

By and large the Dutch dress informally for business, though dark suits are not unknown and may be seen as a mark of respect towards colleagues and associates. The Netherlands is perhaps the one country in Europe where it is safe to dress casually for business, though this should not subsequently be seen as an excuse for sloppy or ill-prepared work. The Dutch are open, honest and hardworking and expect others to be the same. Casual dress is acceptable – casual manners and a casual approach to the task in hand are not. The Dutch abhor lateness.

Business visitors are unlikely to receive the lavish entertainment offered in the United States. Work takes place at the office, not at business lunches or over drinks in a wine bar or restaurant. The family is a private institution – business associates are seldom taken home. It is, however, permissible to telephone outside business hours if a problem arises. The Dutch don't leave their work at the office.

Humour

The Dutch are used to the British sense of humour – they see a great deal of it on television – but they do not necessarily share it. They prefer humour to arise naturally from the occasion rather than be artificially inserted into it. It is best not to overplay the comedy card in the Netherlands, and to give our wit something of a rest.

SPAIN

Background

Until quite recently, Spain suffered from its glorious past. Four or five hundred years ago, Spain was the richest and most powerful nation in the world, and it has taken a long time to forget this. When the glory faded, there was much internal rancour and the search for who was to blame almost tore the country to pieces irreparably. In the 19th century, under the ruling Hapsburgs, Spain lost its colonies and much of its pride. The republic was proclaimed in 1931, and the Spanish Civil War which followed lasted from 1936 to 1939. In the bitterest civil war in modern European history, the military, the political right and the Catholic Church joined forces under General Franco (with help from fascists in Germany and Italy) against the Popular Front, an uneasy coalition of republicans, anti-clericals, anarchists, socialists, Communists and Basque and Catalan separatists (with help from the USSR). The Popular Front was defeated, and Franco ruled a fascist state until his death in 1975. The monarchy was restored in the same year, and the first modern democratic elections took place in Spain in 1977.

Politically, Spain is now a stable democracy, though there are still rumblings of discontent, particularly from the militant Basques in the north east, and elections are almost as frequent in Spain as they are in Italy. Spain is still a predominantly Catholic country, though less than 20% of the population regularly go to church. Spain is roughly twice the size of Britain, but has a population roughly two thirds the size. Most industry is situated in the north of the country. The south relies on agriculture and tourism for much of its income. It is important for outsiders to be aware at all times of the desire for increasing autonomy that is felt by most of the regions of Spain – Galicia, Catalonia, Navarre, etc.

Bosses and workers
Traditionally, the Spanish have always been suspicious of government officials, landowners and employers, all of whom they suspect of corruption and dishonesty. This does not help labour relations in Spain. Although the older major industries (iron and steel, shipbuilding, etc.) are largely nationalised, most Spanish business companies are privately owned. The relatively low wages paid to many workers in Spain has attracted much foreign investment, so that although a firm may seem very much a family affair, the family itself has limited control.

In general, the structure of Spanish industry and commerce is going through a period of considerable change. The old authoritarian methods of control and management are disappearing, to be replaced by more modern methods, most of them imported from the United States. This process has caused considerable conflict between younger and older generations. The move is towards more worker participation in the management of companies, but it is a slow process. Companies employing more than fifty workers are obliged by law to set up a works council, and firms with over five hundred employees have to take at least one worker on to the board.

Even with such opportunities for consultation, however, Spanish companies are led from the top. The Chief Executive (almost always a man) will expect his orders to be obeyed, no matter how obscurely they may be issued. There are still many running Spanish businesses with the attitudes of grandees or *hidalgos*. Teamwork is unknown except in companies newly created or run by foreign managers. It is best for outsiders to show respect for the system they find in operation in Spain. The old Spanish business school regards criticism as rudeness.

Relations between the Spanish trade unions, the Spanish government and employers are generally poor. In 1988 the socialist UGT federation overturned the arrangement between the three whereby they met regularly to determine the level of national pay settlements. Since then Spain has moved increasingly towards a market led economy, and, with a high level of unemployment and relatively low welfare spending, the gap between bosses and workers has tended to widen.

Business practice

There are those who have found Spanish business practices lacking in reliability – in terms of delivery dates, quality control, regularity of supply, etc. It pays to check and double check, and regular visits to business associates are advisable. Since the Spanish are an extremely hospitable people, this usually presents no problem.

Meetings are seen as opportunities to pass on decisions that have already been taken, rather than as forums for discussion. The one advantage of this system is that meetings tend, therefore, to be short. Again, the exceptions to these generalisations are those firms that have introduced more modern management methods. Otherwise, those who seek to gain promotion by showing outstanding ability and bright ideas are doomed to disappointment. Loyalty rather than brilliance is prized in Spanish business culture.

Informality

The Spanish tend to be informal in their relationships with business associates. Suits are uncommon in the office – jacket and trousers are the norm, and the jacket may be removed readily. In their business dress, the Spanish are much more like the French than the Germans. At first it may be wise to use 'Senor' or 'Senora' followed by the family name, but the likelihood is that the Spanish themselves will early seek to use first names in conversation. Unlike France, Germany and Italy, manners tend to be more formal in the south than in the north.

The Spanish are unlikely to be punctual, but the *manana* approach may have had its day, or its tomorrow.

Social arrangements

The Spanish like to meet ostensibly to conduct business over lunch or dinner. It is in settings such as bars and restaurants that many decisions are reached which will ultimately be conveyed to junior management and the workforce, but it may take several courses to reach the point where business is at last discussed.

The Spanish are proud of their families. To be invited to a Spanish home should be regarded as an honour, and we should never do anything to upset family pride.

Humour

The Spanish love humour, but jokes that are intended to prick a person's pride are out of place in Spain. It is said that the pun does not exist in Spain. Only those of us with extremely good Spanish or Catalan should attempt to put this theory to the test.

CHAPTER 20

Japanese business etiquette

There is no such thing in Japan as a real 'working' luncheon or dinner. Foreign visitors with high hopes of clinching a contract are invariably disappointed with what they consider their counterparts' evasiveness throughout the meal. The purpose of the business luncheon is to enhance a sense of intimacy and to serve as a lubricant for present or future negotiations.

NISSAN MOTOR COMPANY

Hito no kokoro wa yoru wakaru
(You get through to a man's soul at night)
Japanese saying, quoted in *Business in Japan*
ed. NORBURY AND BOWNAS 1974

Background

For some fifteen hundred years, until 1945, the dominant religion of Japan was Shintoism, a religion which has no founding figure but is based upon worship of ancestors and a belief in the divine powers of natural forces. The Japanese worshipped their god-emperor, head of state and religion, a man with divine powers. Although it was formally disestablished by the American occupying forces after the Second World War and adherence to Shintoism has declined in modern Japan, Japanese culture is still much influenced by it. There are even signs of a revival of interest in the faith by those who feel that Japanese society has become too 'worldly'.

The Japanese islands were the home of the Ainu aboriginal people, but have long been subject to invasion and influence from outside. In the 7th century, the islands were occupied by the Chinese, who established a strong centralised kingdom based on Chinese institutions. For the next six hundred years Japan developed independently with a series of *shogun*, hereditary military rulers who held the country under tight feudal control. From 1192 to 1867 Japan was ruled only nominally by an emperor – real power lay in the hands of the *shogun*. They were powerful enough to withstand an attempted invasion by Genghis Khan in 1281. In the 16th century Vasco da Gama reached Japan, and Nagasaki became an important trading post with Europeans (especially the Dutch) and others.

In the late 16th century, Japan was reunified by a strong ruler, Hideyoshi Toyotomi, who was one of the first Japanese to seek an overseas empire. He invaded and conquered Korea, and piratical raids were launched against China. In the mid 17th century, the Japanese adopted an insular outlook. Christian missionaries were banned from the country, the Japanese were forbidden to travel abroad, and foreign contacts were limited to those with the Dutch, the Chinese and the Koreans. Nevertheless, Japan became increasingly prosperous, and the population rose from 20 million in 1600 to 30 million a little over one hundred years later (at the same time the population of Britain rose from 5 million to just over 8 million).

By the beginning of the 19th century, Japan was prosperous and well-governed, with a high degree of literacy and an intensive agricultural system. The Japanese were well prepared to meet western expansion in the north Pacific. Ships from Russia, France, Britain and the United States called at Nagasaki, Edo (now Tokyo) and Hakodate, seeking trade. Links with western ideas and news of the California Gold Rush of 1849 prompted a wave of emigration from Japan to the United States in the mid 19th century.

Japanese isolation was ended by the demands of the United States, among others, to have access to Japanese ports. In 1858 'unequal treaties' were concluded under threats from western powers. These treaties led to the fall of the Tokugawa dynasty, and in 1868 the Meiji imperial dynasty was restored, to oversee a period of rapid industrialisation. The new leaders of Japan saw the necessity to pursue national wealth as a means of asserting Japan's international independence. Feudalism and Samurai privileges were abolished and a central bureaucracy was established. In the 1870s a conscript army was created and a navy was founded, equipped with modern warships. By 1900 90% of school age children were in school.

Despite poor natural resources such as coal, iron ore and oil, Japan was the only non-western society to build a broad and varied industrial base by the early 20th century. Capitalism made rapid headway in Japan. While the major nations of Europe were at war from 1914 to 1918, Japanese penetration of foreign markets quickly increased. By 1918 the population of Japan had risen to 55 million. In 1929 Japanese industry produced a net income of $1000 million, an amount comparable to that of Canada and two and a half times that of Australia. Official encouragement was given to industry by quality control of export goods (e.g. silk), subsidies or direct government investment in strategic and import-saving industries, technical training schemes, tax advantages and better transport and communication systems.

The second half of the 19th century saw an increasingly assertive Japanese foreign policy. Japan coveted Korea, Formosa and stretches of the Chinese mainland. The Ogasawara islands, to the south east of mainland Japan, were annexed in 1873 with the tacit approval of Britain and the United States. Two years later the entire chain of Kurile islands (between Japan and the United States) were ceded to Japan. The Ryukyu islands were claimed from China in 1879. In 1894 Japan went to war with China and gained the province of Taiwan. Ten years later, victory in the Russo-Japanese War brought Japanese rights in southern Manchuria. In 1910 the Japanese annexed Korea and later extended their rights in Manchuria and in the Chinese province of Shantung.

It had been a lively and prosperous fifty years of Meiji rule, during which time imports and exports had both risen by over 2000%. Imports were now largely raw materials rather than finished goods, and Japan had become a major investment centre for European colonial powers outside Europe. But in 1918 the Japanese army began to act independently and traditionalists denounced what they saw as the 'westernisation' of Japan.

The western recessions of the 1920s and 1930s had disastrous results for Japan. The Japanese were excluded from many world markets and saw this as a deliberate policy of racism on the part of the west. The Depression hit Japan very hard. People became disillusioned with party government. Economic decline at home led to increasing power being assumed by the military, and in the 1930s Japan embarked on another period of military conquest. From 1937 to 1939 the Japanese conquered much of north east China and Manchuria. A New Order was proclaimed – western powers were to be driven from Asia. A United States economic boycott of Japan was swiftly followed by the Japanese attack on Pearl Harbour and the outbreak of war between Japan and the US.

The war cost Japan dear, but post-war reconstruction was swift. From 1945 to 1952 Japan was occupied by the Allies under United States supervision – it was not until 1972 that Okinawa was once again placed under full Japanese control. The major Japanese economic and industrial recovery took place between 1952 and 1974, by which time Japan had become the third-largest industrial power in the world.

Geography and economy
Japan is an archipelago made up of four main islands – Honshu, Hokkaido, Kyushu and Shikoku. It is separated from mainland Asia by the Sea of Japan, and from the United States by the vast waters of the Pacific Ocean. It is roughly one and a half times the size of Britain, but has twice the population. It is a mountainous country, with active volcanoes and frequent earthquakes. It is still one of the most intensively cultivated lands in the world.

But modern Japan is almost synonymous with modern industry. Many of the giant industrial names of the 1970s,

1980s and 1990s are Japanese – Honda, Nissan, Toshiba, Sony, JVC, Toyota, etc. etc. In the past ten years, the Japanese have increasingly successfully exported not only their goods, but also their technology and work ethic. Familiarity with Japanese practices does not lead to contempt, but may result in an assumed awareness with how the Japanese work. We tend to have a series of flash-cards in our heads – of workers limbering up for the day's work with a session of physical exercises, of directors of Japanese companies sitting next to members of the workforce in factory canteens, of complete mastery over and adoption of western business methods.

It can sometimes be a case of a little learning being a dangerous thing, for Japanese business etiquette requires careful study.

NOTE ON LANGUAGE: Japanese appears to be unrelated to any other language, though its grammar is similar to Korean, and the roots of its written script lie in the Chinese characters of the 3rd and 4th centuries. Modern phonetic letters and characters have been adopted since 1945.

Introduction to Japanese business etiquette

For all the bright lights, fast food outlets, golf courses, western style of greeting by handshake and other western influences, the Japanese are a traditional, reserved people who maintain and enjoy many of the social and business formalities of the past. Like the French, they admire and appreciate efforts on the part of foreigners to show a willingness to adapt to their ways, but this should not be overdone. If a foreigner makes himself or herself look foolish by trying to appear too Japanese, then the Japanese themselves will be embarrassed by the foreigner's loss of face. Plain old-fashioned courtesy and politeness, and an absence of assertiveness, will usually be enough on the part of any visitor to establish cordial relations, for the Japanese do not make the same distinction between social and business behaviour that we do.

The key to good business relations with any Japanese is the

establishment of good personal relations. A business associate is seen as a friend, and that includes, ultimately, a visitor from overseas. In this relationship, it is important to understand that the Japanese tend to take an emotional rather than an intellectual stance. They are proud of the friendships that they have established during their business careers, and place a high value on them. For much of their entire history, their relationships with the rest of the world have been uneasy, and there is still what amounts almost to an inferiority complex present when the Japanese compare their own lifestyle with that of most western nations. They are aware of their tremendous industrial, technical and commercial achievements in their own modest way, but they are also aware of the cramped and polluted conditions in which many of them live. Anyone who has seen station staff cramming commuters into trains during the rush hour in Tokyo will know that such behaviour would not go down too well at Paddington in the early evening.

Business practice
For good or ill, the Japanese still have a reputation in the west as being great developers of other people's ideas. They are not great innovators. They like to follow, and improve on, an existing practice. As soon as the first Japanese company had set up a factory in Europe to produce Japanese goods, others swiftly followed. The main implication of this approach is that the Japanese take a long time to get used to a radically new idea. We should not expect them to come to snap decisions or show immediate enthusiasm for a concept or a practice that they are not used to.

In business, the Japanese prefer collective rather than individual decision making. Discussions are long and frequent. It is important to reach a consensus, no matter how difficult this may be. It's not often that one figure emerges in a Japanese company as a 'whizz-kid' or the guiding genius of a new project. It's more likely that one person will have the power to veto a new proposal than push it through. In any business dealings with a Japanese company, therefore, it is vital to consult as many people as possible, to give the impression that we respect the opinion of all our Japanese colleagues.

The art of negotiating, Japanese style

Although the Japanese respect tough negotiating, they expect it to be accompanied by a strong personal relationship. Negotiations do not take place between rivals or enemies, but among friends. To understand this better, it is necessary to know something of two pairs of Japanese concepts – *on* and *giri*, *honne* and *tatemae*. *On* and *giri* refer to the senses of obligation and duty that the Japanese still feel among themselves in business dealings. *Honne* and *tatemae*, perhaps the more important pair, refer to the inner feelings experienced during the negotiations, and the outer presentation of those feelings, which may be almost mask-like. More specifically, *honne* describes the underlying motive behind the stance taken or the view expressed, the real intention behind what is being said. *Tatemae* describes the face that is put on, the formal facade, the front face.

To the Japanese there is no sense of duplicity whatsoever in these two concepts. The front face preserves a continuity within the relationship. It is unruffled. It shows respect for the relationship. The Japanese are often surprised and hurt at the absence of this dual approach on the part of westerners. When it was announced that the German firm BMW were taking over Rover Cars in January 1994, Nobuhiko Kawamoto, the President of Honda, who already owned a 20% share in the company and were seeking to extend that, was clearly unhappy. It was not only that he felt that the deal went against his company's interests. He was also hurt by the absence of *tatemae* on the part of Rover and the British Government and press. It was all very well for all three to be delighted inside, but their exterior deportment should have been more sensitive, hiding that delight behind a calm exterior.

Two other words reveal more about the art of negotiation in

225

Japan – *hai* and *ma*. *Hai* sometimes simply means 'yes', but it also has a subtler meaning in negotiations, giving an indication that the listener has heard what is being said. It should not be taken as a sign of agreement, therefore, but only as interest in the discussion at hand. *Ma* really means nothing at all, but is thrown into a conversation or a discussion as a means of playing for time. Once uttered, it allows whoever said it time for thought – a verbal version of time-out in basketball.

Entertaining and being entertained
There are a few signs that the Japanese policy of avoiding business lunches, quoted at the top of this chapter, may be changing, but for the moment the vast majority of Japanese do not see lunchtime as a time for doing business, or for getting so drunk that business is impossible. Any drinking at lunchtime will be limited to a single toast (*kampai*). Entertaining is therefore confined to the evenings, and, since most Japanese live a long way from their offices, it is rare for a visitor to be invited into a Japanese home for an evening meal.

Most entertaining takes place in restaurants. It is wisest to allow our Japanese hosts to choose what to eat, unless, of course, we have strongly held vegetarian or other dietary views (which will be respected, but it isn't a good idea to embark on a passionate attack on whaling). The Japanese are happy to drink alcohol on such occasions, and it is not considered bad manners to appear slightly tipsy (paralytically drunk is another matter).

It is also a good idea to take our lead from Japanese hosts when it comes to the formal seating arrangements for a meal or a meeting. There are two types of seating plan for such occasions – the formal and the very formal. At formal gatherings, guests and hosts all sit round a single table, but each stay together in single groups – there is no mixing of the two. At very formal gatherings, each guest and each host sits at a separate table, the chief host first standing in the centre of the room to welcome the guests individually. The very formal gathering tends to be the first of the series – *ichijikai*.

Subsequent meetings or gatherings are called *nijikai*. It is a mark of honour to proceed to the *nijikai* stage, proof that we have successfully got over the first hurdle, the *ichijikai*. When we issue a reciprocal invitation to repay the Japanese hospitality, we have to go back to square one, back to *ichijikai*, back to extreme formality. Distinguishing between the two is not as difficult as it may sound, for they take place in different locations. *Nijikai* always follows *ichijikai* at an informal drinking club. At either occasion, the place of honour is usually that furthest from the entrance to the room or nearest to the *tokonoma*, an alcove set in one of the walls in which scrolls are hung and flower arrangements are placed. Traditionally, it is considered correct to refuse the position of honour even if it is being offered, but this approach requires a reasonable knowledge of Japanese etiquette if it is to be carried off with conviction. Most of us will fare better by modestly accepting the position of honour.

The younger generation of Japanese no longer adopt the old way of sitting on the heels for meetings or when being entertained in a restaurant, which is just as well for most westerners. But we should take our lead from our Japanese hosts when it comes to when and where we should respectfully remove our shoes, and it is still *de rigueur* to sit cross-legged or with legs stretched out on the *tatami* mat. At all costs we should avoid giving the impression that we are slouching.

The third stage of entertaining is *karaoke*, which means exactly what it means at the local in Britain, though it does help if our repertoire is not limited to *My Way* and Beatles standards. *Karaoke* is Japanese for 'empty orchestra', and is extremely popular. We should expect to be invited to sing, and, no matter how poor the voice, attempts to do so will be applauded. Similarly, if we are invited to play golf while in Japan (a sporting obsession for many Japanese), we should accept, no matter how bad the handicap.

When returning hospitality in Japan care must be taken not to invite Japanese representatives who are in positions senior to our own. This is considered a grave breach of etiquette.

Only a President should invite another President. If we wish to offer hospitality to a Japanese who holds a position above our own, then we have to persuade our own senior representative to do so. For a long time the Japanese loathed the cocktail party, but accepted it as it was the western way of entertaining. Older Japanese still find something abhorrent about the notion of eating and drinking while standing up.

Women in Japan
Although wives of visiting foreigners will almost always be included in invitations to meals or receptions, Japanese wives will probably not be present on such occasions. Apart from any *geisha* or hostesses, therefore, it is possible that a visiting wife will be the only female present. Japanese women do not expect to be paid the polite attention that is regarded as good manners in western society.

Gifts
It is customary in Japan to give presents to business colleagues who are visiting the country, and the Japanese expect similar gifts in return. These gifts should be small, symbolic, representative of company or country – go for quality rather than quantity. Scotch whisky is very acceptable to Japanese men, but we show more care and respect if we give a good malt whisky rather than the more popular and cheaper brands – most of which are readily obtainable in Japan. A more suitable gift for a woman may be a small ornament or piece of china. What matters also is the way the gift is wrapped and presented. Again, like the French, the Japanese like their presents to be lavishly wrapped and decorated. The present should be handed over with due ceremony, no muttered 'just a little something I saw at the airport . . .'

The gift will remain wrapped when handed over unless whoever gives it indicates that it is to be opened there and then. Such gifts should always be treated with great reverence. When leaving Japan, after, say, a series of negotiations, it is customary to give a present to the head of the company with whom we have been dealing, even if we have seen very little of him (or, exceptionally, her).

Name cards

The Japanese always expect to exchange business cards at the first meeting. This is not just an expression of politeness – it is seen as an essential way of establishing name and position within a company immediately. This is important as it reveals the hierarchy of all those taking part in discussions or negotiations.

These cards should be in both English and Japanese, clearly showing in both languages, name, rank and company address. The Japanese needs to be faultless, to avoid any misunderstandings, and is best checked by an expert. It is not considered rude to spend some time examining these cards, to learn who's who in the business at hand. If anything is unclear, it is correct to ask for clarification. It is also important to note very carefully the position each person holds within a company. The head of a Japanese company is not usually the Chairperson. He or she will be seen as a semi-retired official. The active head of any company is the president, not the managing director as in some British companies. These cards may also be exchanged at receptions, dinners or on other social occasions. Wherever and whenever we are offered a business card by a Japanese, we should be ready to offer one of our own cards in return.

One of the gravest breaches of business etiquette in Japan is to put on airs and graces, to pretend to be of higher rank than we really are. The Japanese have great respect for position, and are therefore shocked when they discover that someone has attempted to gain extra *kudos* by claiming to be more important than is subsequently discovered to be the truth.

CHAPTER 21

Korean Business Etiquette

At 15 I set my heart on learning; at 30 I was firmly established; at 40 I had no more doubts; at 50 I knew the will of Heaven; at 60 I was ready to listen to it; at 70 I could follow my heart's desire without transgressing what was right.

CONFUCIUS (towards the end of his life 551–479 BC)

As the standard of living improves in Korea, we shall eventually lose the stage of working hard. Until we get to that stage, we shall have to keep our economy growing.

WOO-CHOONG KIM, founder of the
Daewoo Business Empire (to employees in 1983)

Background

Although Korea has been a national state for over 2000 years, the country has undergone a stormy and unsettled history for much of that time. Up to the 7th century AD, Korea consisted of three kingdoms – Koguryo, Paekche and Shilla. None of these kingdoms was strong enough to withstand a succession of invasions by the Chinese, but in the 7th century, Shilla overthrew the other two kingdoms and united the whole Korean peninsula. For seven hundred years the Koryo dynasty ruled Korea in what may be regarded as a golden age. The arts flourished, Buddhism became the most popular religion, and Korea was centuries ahead of Europe in scientific and technical development. The printing press with movable metal type existed in Korea long before it was developed in Germany.

In 1392 the Koryo dynasty was ousted by the Yi dynasty. Buddhism was replaced by Confucianism as the leading religion. For almost three hundred years Korea still remained an independent state, but Japan was emerging in the Far East as a formidable power. Three times in fifteen years the Japanese under Hideyoshi Toyotami invaded Korea. The Koreans were supported by the Chinese but paid a price for this support. Invasions by Manchu armies in 1627, 1636 and 1637 led to Korea becoming a vassal state of China in 1637.

As China became increasingly weak in the 18th and 19th centuries, Korea regained independence, but was again invaded by Japan early in the 20th century, and officially annexed in 1910. It was also used as a base from which Japan could attack Russia during the Russo-Japanese War of 1904–5. Japanese rule lasted until 1945 and the period is remembered with bitterness by many of the older generation of Koreans. The Koreans are a traditional people, always reluctant to admit sudden change, and Japanese attempts to set aside Korean culture and language were resisted and resented.

During the Second World War, to foster Korean resistance to Japanese rule, the United States, Britain, China and the USSR promised to restore Korean independence once Japan had been defeated. The effect of this promise was to establish a divided Korea in 1948. The dividing line was the 38th parallel – south of the line was placed under American control, north of the line was placed under Soviet control. In the same year, North Korea was proclaimed as the People's Democratic Republic of Korea, and an independent constitution was framed for the Republic of South Korea.

The division between the two halves of Korea was politically as basic as could be. The north developed along communist lines, and the south followed the pattern of an emerging western democracy. The ideological split still exists today. From time to time there appears hope of rapprochement between the two countries, but such times are interspersed with periods of worsening relations and the occasional threat of outright war.

War did break out between North and South Korea in 1950, after the withdrawal of US and USSR forces, when troops from the North Korean army crossed the 38th parallel. The United Nations authorised military assistance for South Korea, and, after three years of bitter fighting, the war ended with neither side emerging victorious. In the uneasy truce that has followed (for North and South Korea are still technically at war – only an armistice was signed at Panmunjon in 1953), both North and South Korea have become prosperous countries, more so than any other Far Eastern countries save Japan, Malaysia, Taiwan and the Philippines.

This chapter is concerned with business practice and etiquette in the Republic of South Korea.

Politics

Since 1953 South Korea has experienced many political changes. In 1961 a military coup overthrew the attempt to establish a workable parliamentary government. There followed a period of martial law under a harsh authoritarian regime. In 1980 attempts were resumed to establish constitutional government. By October 1987 the popular demand for this had become insistent, and a new constitution was introduced, with universal suffrage, a reduction in the length of a presidency from seven to five years and considerable curtailment of the President's powers. Korea's first free presidential election since 1971 was held on 16th December 1987 and was won by Roh Tae Woo. President Roh did much to improve relations between South and North Korea and other Communist countries, but reunification of Korea remains unlikely for the foreseeable future. At present, following the elections of December 1992, the President is Kim Yung Sam of the ruling Democratic Liberal Party.

Partly by reason of the military assistance given to the Republic of South Korea by British troops during the Korean War, South Korea maintains good relations with Britain.

Geography and economy

The Republic of South Korea is roughly two-fifths the size of Britain, but has a population of almost 40 million people. It is a mountainous country bordered on the west by the Yellow Sea and on the east by the Sea of Japan. The western side of the peninsula is less mountainous than the east. The soil is generally poor and only some 20% of the land is arable. Winters are cold, summers are very hot and wet. The capital is Seoul. The main ports are Inchon and Pusan. The southern tip of the Japanese island of Honshu is only some hundred miles from Pusan.

The Korean peninsula itself is some 600 miles long (the South Korean section approximately half of this). Along the 38th parallel is a Demilitarized Zone some two and a half miles wide. Communications in the Republic of South Korea are good. There is a well-established road network, by which it's possible to reach any part of the country within a day. The major cities are connected by a fast railroad system. There are three international airports in Korea, at Seoul (in the north), Pusan (in the south east) and Cheju (a separate island, roughly seventy miles south of mainland Korea).

Until the second half of the 20th century there was an economic divide between North and South Korea. Most industry had been situated in the north, the south being largely an agricultural area. This left the Republic of South Korea with little in the way of natural resources after partition. With enormous aid from the United States, however, the south Koreans rapidly began to build an industrial base (shipbuilding, textile and steel industries), and South Korea today is the world's twelfth largest trading nation. The *per capita* GNP has risen by some 7000% in the last thirty years. South Korea has also moved from reliance on the older, labour-intensive industries to modern high tech industries.

Korea's main two markets are the United States and Japan. The Korean protectionist approach to trade (imports are seen as 'bad') has led to some embarrassment in negotiations with the United States, who wish to see Korean import barriers removed. Korea is committed to conform to OECD tariffs by the mid 1990s, and, partly to compensate for this, is looking for more trade with Europe in the immediate future. Korea has an imbalance of trade with the Japanese, who supply most of Korea's imports. At present, Korea trades more with Germany than any other European country.

The giants of Korean industry are known as the Chaebol, the top ten companies that control some 50% of Korea's exports. The best known members of the Chaebol are probably Samsung, Hyundai, Sangyong, Sunkyong and Lucky Goldstar. There are signs that the Korean government is seeking to develop a network of more small and medium sized companies.

Business practice and etiquette
The Koreans are by nature kind and hospitable people. They have a great desire to please and are extremely honest. They expect and admire sincerity in others. But they are also, to western eyes, blunt, crude, superstitious and aggressive (a law was passed in the early 15th century making it compulsory for Koreans to wear heavy pottery hats – this was an attempt to make fights in the streets impossible).

They are a formal and traditional people who do not wish to see their own culture brushed aside by what many of them regard as invasive western ways. The pace of change in Korea has been staggering in the last twenty or thirty years, but many of the traditional ways are respected. It is still considered bad manners to make contact unannounced, i.e. without a formal introduction from a mutual third party. Indeed, it is unlikely that we should be able to make the acquaintance of those Koreans we wish to meet without such formal introduction. Unsolicited mail, unheralded and speculative visits are not appreciated in Korea. The correct way to approach a business company is to ask a third party to make contact and to act as an intermediary. Care should be taken in choosing this intermediary – the amount of respect in which he or she is held will decide the amount of respect in which we ourselves are held. It is important, therefore, to do some homework before making contact.

Once the initial contact has been made, it is important to

maintain regular and frequent contact. This applies at all levels within a company. It is incorrect in Korea to assume that we should have dealings only with the most senior member of the Korean company. Some British and American business visitors to Korea have found that daily contact with their Korean partners should be established wherever possible. This is because personnel changes are frequent in most Korean companies, and the person with whom we dealt last week may well have moved on (sideways, upwards or downwards – it is a volatile business society) and been replaced by someone else. Also, it is a mistake to take a business relationship for granted once it has been established. Personal visits are always welcome, and we shouldn't hesitate to make them. Frequent progress reports are expected on any deals that have been struck. All this may take time, for although the Koreans leap into action once it is time to implement the terms of a contract, they like to linger over their business deals, much as the Arabs do.

Formality of business life
Koreans love hierarchy and authority. This is due to the cultural influence of Confucianism, which teaches five superior-subordinate relationships: ruler and subject, father and son, husband and wife, elder and younger brother, friend and friend. Loyalty is a key element of Korean society.

This way of thinking provides the backbone of Korean business etiquette. Every person has his or her clearly defined place in the organisation of industry and commerce. That place is known and understood by all, and outsiders should make their own position in their own business society clear from the outset. Great store is therefore set in the way outsiders introduce themselves in Korea. It is essential at all times to carry business cards which display name, company and position within that company. In return for presenting these, we shall be given cards by every Korean to whom we are introduced. The exchange of these cards may be conducted with considerable ceremony, and the cards themselves should be meticulously kept for future reference. There are some 35 million people in the Republic of South Korea, and over half of them are called either Lee (or Yi), Kim, Pak or Choi. So, no offence will be taken if we show that we have to refer to these subsequently, say, at a meeting.

The Koreans are themselves most respectful towards high-ranking business executives and highly qualified technicians. They see both as the embodiments of an important wisdom, and as teachers in the traditional sense. A high position in the business world is equated with a high position in society, the basis of what amounts almost to an aristocracy.

Language

Many Koreans find it as difficult to learn English as we do to learn Korean, and their knowledge of English may not be as competent as it appears at first hearing. It is important, therefore, not to assume that a Korean has understood what we have said in English, even if it appears all is well. Korean courtesy may inhibit them from asking us to repeat what we have said or to express it in some other terms so that they may better understand. This may also be true of those Koreans who are acting as interpreters.

Those westerners who have taken the trouble to learn some Korean gain respect, but it takes two or three months' hard work to become fluent. The Koreans are proud of their language, and, indeed, of their whole culture. They do not see themselves as 'alternative Japanese'. To Koreans, it was the Japanese who borrowed and learnt from Korea, not the other way round.

Like their society, the Korean language is structured on several levels. The highest level is the language that is used towards superiors, the language of respect. Then there is the familiar and friendly language that is used towards close friends and equals. Lastly, there is the rougher language, that used to inferiors. Anyone who wishes to converse in depth in Korean needs to learn all three levels, and never make the mistake of using the wrong one.

237

Negotiations

Korean business is conducted with some ceremony, from the moment of *hwangyong hoe*, or 'welcome', onwards. Negotiations are slow and dignified. It is considered a breach of etiquette to attempt to push or hurry things along. The hard sell is definitely not welcomed in Korea, but Koreans respect a firm attitude, held and expressed with patience and politeness. If there is a genuine desire on the part of Korean associates to come to a business agreement, then this desire will eventually be fulfilled. A common practice in Korea is to leave minor details or smaller bones of contention to be dealt with by others, intermediaries or go-betweens. If such a wish becomes apparent, we should bow to it, though not literally, and delegate such matters to our own intermediaries. It can be a little disconcerting, however, to discover that the Koreans are quite happy to agree the broad principle of a deal, in a contract, and then leave the terms of that contract to be settled after the contract has been signed.

Although the chief executive or managing director of a Korean firm may well appear not to be troubled by committing details of negotiations to paper, it may be wise to do so from our own point of view. Telephone conversations can often be misunderstood, when at least one side is negotiating in a foreign tongue. It is best to confirm what has been said on the phone in writing, as soon as possible.

All this may take a considerable amount of time, and we have to be patient. The modern methods that prevail on Korean assembly lines and in Korean hi-tech factories are not reflected in Korean ways of doing business. Reaching agreement on the terms of a contract can be a slow and painful process, though it will always be conducted with great politeness. It is ill-mannered to appear exasperated in Korean society, no matter how much longer a meeting is taking than we thought it would. We have to respect the Korean tradition of taking decisions collectively.

People, not paper

Another reason why a considerable amount of time may have to be spent in negotiations with Koreans is that they are more interested in the people with whom they are negotiating than the printed outcome of the negotiation itself. Once they feel they have established the right degree of mutual trust, Koreans are prepared to sign contracts that cover the broad outline of the agreement reached, leaving the finer details to be arranged at some later date, possibly by other representatives. They prefer this approach to having to sweat through a contract that covers every eventuality. Koreans have considerable faith in the integrity of people they have got to know.

The corollary of this is that it is the height of bad manners to question the integrity of a Korean or to manipulate a situation so that a Korean is forced to take a certain action that he or she dislikes. Attempting to put pressure on a Korean is ill-advised. The Koreans respond to praise and to feelings of goodwill generally. They are conscious of their own *kibun* or inner happiness, and, if this is well established, business dealings can become good-natured affairs. Above all, we must ensure that we never place Korean partners, clients or colleagues in positions where they may lose face. This would be considered unforgivable.

In all this, it helps if we do our homework and find out as much as we can about the people with whom we are dealing. Koreans are flattered by such knowledge. This may sound a little cold-blooded and calculating, but to know the position held in society, the birthday, the family background, and something of the basic philosophy of a Korean colleague is seen as a mark of honour and respect. The Koreans are very conscious of 'standing' and the esteem in which they are held by others. Evincing interest is taken as a compliment.

The Korean language itself reveals the importance of 'face' and inner peace or *kibun*. Crucial elements of Korean negotiations are *achom*, 'compliments' or 'flattery', and *chansa*, which also means compliments. Koreans dislike being the bearers of unpleasant news as this, they feel, adversely affects

239

a person's *kibun*. Their reluctance to do this may complicate business negotiations from time to time. It can also lead to tampering with published business accounts to avoid showing a loss at the end of a year's trading, which would, of course, lead to further loss of *kibun*.

Loyalty in Korea is more to the individual who owns or runs the company (or department) than to the company itself. The working day usually begins with the ceremony of *chohoe*, which expresses this loyalty. All this has repercussions for business negotiations. The Koreans are more interested in expressing loyalty in business deals than in reaching what westerners would regard as a fair compromise. This is why their negotiating stance may sometimes appear aggressive.

The pace of change in Korea
Change is underway at a frantic pace in Korean industry and business. The Republic of South Korea has moved in under fifty years from being a predominantly agrarian community using traditional farming methods to a modern commercial society with heavy investment in communication and electronics industries. The *per capita* income has increased enormously, and with this increase have come dramatic changes in the lifestyle of most of the population. Consumerism is rife. The Koreans eat, play, dress and house themselves 'western style'. It's a mistake to regard all this as an indication that they have lost touch with their traditional culture, however. For all the bustle and excitement of business life that is evident in Korea, the Koreans remain faithful to the culture of their ancestors. There is a limit to the extent that western ways are allowed to operate, especially in the business world, and the Korean way of thinking doesn't correspond to western logic. It is more important in Korea to establish a personal empathy with colleagues, based on shared emotional responses and outlook, than to agree on business plans or policy. It may also help to bear in mind that, to the Koreans, the share held in the market, the sheer trading volume of a company, is more important than the size of profit gained.

It may help to see Korea in terms of a mixture of Buddhism and Confucianism. The two were contemporaries in the 7th century BC, but Buddha was a progressive and Confucius was a conservative. Buddhism expounds the 'noble eightfold path' – right views, right thought, plain and truthful speech, moral conduct, application to the task in hand, the correct level of understanding of past and present and future, and contemplation or meditation. Confucianism leads by example. The example set by a ruler or elder influences all his subjects – the concept of 'her' does not enter into this. Rulers must be faultless in their etiquette, behaving with lofty courtesy towards their inferiors. Formality is important to the Confucian mind. Ceremonies must be performed with all due care and adherence to protocol, politeness matters at all times and among all people, and duty is of the highest importance.

Given that there has been this dichotomy between Buddhism and Confucianism in Korean society throughout their history, it is not surprising to find a similar dichotomy in Korean business life (on the one hand a traditional set of mind, on the other hand modern hi-tech capacity and methods). The inference to be drawn is that it is essential to show sensitivity to the situation in which we find ourselves. Korea is no place for those who treat people as 'units' or 'numbers'. There is no doubt, however, that the pressures on Koreans to change their ways, and adopt those of the west entirely, are huge and may ultimately prove irresistible. Market economies are remarkably intolerant of old-established ways of doing things.

Entertaining

Anyone doing business in Korea is almost certain to be invited to some form of entertainment or social occasion. Such invitations should always be accepted – to decline an invitation in Korea is to give offence, however unintentionally. Problems may arise, having accepted the invitation, however, as many Korean parties, receptions or dinners involve a considerable amount of heavy drinking. A strong constitution is needed to keep pace with Korean hosts, who see the ability to consume vast quantities of alcohol, at the same time preserving an outward display of good manners and consideration to others, as a sign of honour and trustworthiness.

The Koreans also believe that business dealings should be accompanied by the presentation of small gifts. These are not seen in any way as constituting bribes, or as being attempts to oil the works of busy life. They are simply presentations that indicate respect for their new partners. In turn, they expect reciprocal invitations from those to whom they have given hospitality, and return gifts from those to whom they have given presents.

A great honour in Korea is to be invited to play golf (*kolpu*) with Korean business colleagues. The invitation should always be accepted. It will not matter how bad we are at golf, though the Koreans seem to believe that every Westerner is a potential Faldo or Woosnam.

Handshaking and bowing
Hand-shaking is a perfectly acceptable way of greeting some-one in Korea. Often both hands are used – the right hand is offered first, and the left hand is placed on top of the right, as a mark of affection. Bowing does still exist, however, and is considered appropriate at formal functions, especially towards older Koreans. As we might expect from the stratified nature of Korean society, there are several levels of bow. The deeper the bow, the more respect is being shown. Care should be taken not to give offence by bowing too slightly.

Tipping
Since a 10% service charge is added to almost every bill in Korea, tips are not expected, save in three situations:

1. To porters at airports.
2. To guides, who have rendered exceptional service.
3. To taxi drivers who have also carried luggage etc.

Holidays in Korea

Koreans have a long working day. Most offices are open from 8.30 in the morning until 7.00 at night. Government departments are open from 9.00 in the morning to 6.00 at night in the summer, and from 9.00 in the morning to 5.00 in the evening in the winter, as well as Saturday mornings.

The two main holidays in Korea take place in or around January. Koreans celebrate the western New Year, and it is the custom, from 3 January to 5 January to call on friends, family, clients and customers, in the case of the latter to ask for their continued patronage. This ceremony is known as *seibei*, the 'beginning of the year bow'. The Korean New Year is known as *Minsok Jol*, 'Folklore Day'. Offices and factories are closed, and roads and railways are packed with people travelling to visit their relatives.

A final note . . .

Koreans love singing, and western visitors will be expected to show their own singing skills (*jangki*). It is perhaps a good idea to spend a good deal of time in the bath before we leave for Korea.

CHAPTER 22

Business etiquette in the Arab world

Far are the shades of Arabia,
Where the Princes ride at noon

WALTER DE LA MARE – *Arabia*

We know that this mad dog of the Middle East has a goal of world revolution, Muslim fundamentalist revolution, which is targeted on many of his own Arab compatriots, and where we figure in that I don't know . . .

PRESIDENT RONALD REAGAN
– press conference, 9 April 1986

Background

For many historians, no single event in world history, from the collapse of the Roman Empire to the voyages of discovery at the end of the 15th century and beginning of the 16th century, is more significant than the birth of the prophet Mohammed in AD 570. Islam brought order to the Eurasian heartland after it had been prey to Barbarian raids for hundreds of years.

Mohammed's message was a simple one – that all should submit themselves to the power of God. Although Islam was not initially a proselytising religion, within two hundred years of his death, the message and the faith had spread to cover Arabia, Persia, north Africa, north west India, Armenia, Mesopotamia and Transoxiana (modern Kazakhstan). With the rise of Islam, there was an accompanying increase in the power and sovereignty of the Abbasid Caliphate, the greatest of whom was Haroun al-Rashid (AD 763–809), the Caliph generally associated with *The Arabian Nights*. By the early 9th

245

century, the Caliphate stretched from Libya to the Indus, encompassing Arabia, Persia and much of north Africa.

From 900 to 1500 the caliphs extended their power. The Great Caliphate was criss-crossed by many of the major medieval trade routes: from Samarkand to Baghdad, Tripoli and on to Venice; from Basra to Aleppo, and then across the Black Sea to Khersan; from Damascus to Tripoli, Tunis and Tangier, and on to Granada, Toledo and Barcelona. During this period, the caliphs conquered the whole of Anatolia (modern Turkey), fought off the Crusaders, captured Constantinople, and shook the whole of Christian Europe.

The Islamic world split into three main empires: the Ottoman, covering Turkey, Greece, Transylvania, Moldavia and the Balkans, almost to the gates of Vienna; the Mameluke, covering the Middle East west of the Euphrates, and Egypt; and the Safavid, covering Arabia east of the Euphrates and Iran. The Mameluke Empire was subsequently absorbed into the enormous Ottoman Empire. But the rise of nationalism in the 19th century eroded much of the Ottoman Empire. By 1913, the end of the Balkan Wars, the Ottoman Empire was limited to Turkey and eastern Thrace. Persia had already become an independent kingdom in 1794. Iraq remained an Ottoman province, until unified in 1921 under British occupation.

In the late 19th and early 20th centuries, the European powers (especially Britain and France) adopted a protective attitude towards much of the Middle East, particularly the Suez Canal and the Persian oilfields. Britain long regarded the Middle East as a stepping stone on a possible invasion route to India. After the First World War, European presence in the Middle East increased. Syria made a brief bid for independence under the Hashemite dynasty from 1918 to 1920, but then was placed under French mandate. Lebanon was occupied by the French. In Saudi Arabia, then called the Nejd, a series of conflicts between the Ibn Saud and Ibn Rashid dynasties resulted in victory for the Saudis in 1921. In 1932 Asir, Hasa,

Hejaz and Nejd were joined together to form the kingdom of Saudi Arabia.

The period from 1920 to 1945 saw further upheaval in the Middle East. In Iraq there was friction between the Arabs and the Assyrians, and between the Kurds and the Iraqis. There were risings against the British and French throughout the area, and in Syria there were civil disturbances, often with a religious or ethnic element. Saudi Arabia became an independent kingdom under the Al Saud dynasty from 1926. Although there were many Arabs, Turks and Kurds in Iran, the majority of the people were Persians. Iran became an independent kingdom under the Pehlevi dynasty in 1925.

After the Second World War, the map was once again redrawn. Jordan became a kingdom founded by the union of Transjordan and part of Palestine under the Hashemite dynasty. From 1946 Syria became an independent republic, with a Sunni Muslim majority. For a brief period (1958–1961) Syria was united with Egypt to form the United Arab Republic. Lebanon also became an independent republic, free from French rule, with a mixed population of Sunni, Shi'i and Druze Muslims. From 1921 to the late 1950s Iraq remained a monarchy, but in 1958 a military revolution overthrew the royal family, and the republic was founded.

The Baghdad Pact of 1955 split the Middle East and Arabia into two main camps – those who supported the Pact (Turkey, Iraq, Iran and Pakistan), and those who opposed it (Syria, Jordan, Saudi Arabia and Egypt).

It has, therefore, always been a mistake to think of the Arab world as one entity. Iran, Iraq and Saudi Arabia alone comprise an area roughly half the size of Europe. There are as many different cultures as there are in Europe. There are almost as many different branches of the Muslim faith as there are of the Christian religion. In Lebanon there are as many Maronite Christians as there are Muslims. It is unlikely, therefore, that there should be unanimity of custom, of outlook or of behaviour.

And the last twenty years has done little to advance the

cause of unity or peace. The overthrow of the Shah in Iran and the establishment of an Islamic fundamentalist state in 1979, war between Iran and Iraq, civil war in Lebanon, tension between Jordan and the Palestinians, and the Gulf War have created a region of distrust and armed readiness for the next conflict. Given the lack of political continuity in the Arab world since the days of the Ottoman Empire and the Great Caliphates, and the nature of the Islamic fundamentalist outlook, it is hardly surprising that it appears to western eyes an unstable part of the world.

Geography and economy

Although oil still provides the enormous bulk of the revenue for Saudi Arabia, Iran and Iraq, it is a mistake to think of the Arab world as one huge oilfield. Though most countries of the Middle East speak Arabic (Iran doesn't – the language there is Persian), they have little else in common.

Saudi Arabia is the largest Arab country in size, but with a population of only 8 million. Much of the country is desert. Iran is much more densely populated – three fifths of the size of Saudi Arabia, but with a population of 35 million. It is also a more mountainous country. Iraq is smaller than Iran (one third the size), with a population of 13 million. As well as oil, Iraq produces a great deal of cotton. Syria is smaller than Iraq, with a population of 8 million. It is a fertile country, whose main export is cotton, though much revenue comes to Syria from the Iraqi oil pipeline that crosses the country. Lebanon is a tiny country by comparison, not much bigger than Cyprus, and with a population of only 3 million. It is in many ways the most European of all Arab countries, fertile, agricultural, beautiful, and torn apart.

Religious customs and holidays

Muslims are called to prayer five times each day – at dawn, midday, mid afternoon, sunset, and approximately one and a half hours after sunset. These sessions of prayer take half an hour and during this time most shops will close and work cease in offices. The exact times of prayer vary from month to month and from country to country, so it is advisable to check times of prayer in local papers, to avoid giving offence by ignoring them. Praying regularly is one of the five basic duties of Islam. The others are:

1. Saying once in one's life, with absolute conviction, 'There is no God but Allah and Mohammed is His Prophet.'
2. Giving alms generously and making provision for the poor.
3. Making the pilgrimage to Mecca at least once in one's life, and
4. Keeping the fast of Ramadan.

The best-known festival in the Muslim calendar, as far as westerners are concerned, is Ramadan, the ninth month of the Muslim year, a time when it is forbidden to eat, drink or smoke from sunrise to sunset. Ramadan ends with the three day festival of Id Al-Fitr in April. Other main festivals are Id Al-Adha (a four-day pilgrimage to Mecca in June), Al Hijra (the Islamic New Year in July), Milad al-Nabi (the anniversary of Mohammed in September) and Lailat Al-Isra wa Al-Mi'raj (celebration of the Prophet's flight to heaven). Visitors to an Arab country should also be aware that Friday is the Muslim holy day and that no business is conducted on that day. In countries such as Lebanon, it is also common for offices to be closed on Sundays.

There are strict Muslim rules concerning diet. The Koran lays down which foods the faithful are allowed to eat (*halal*), and which they must refrain from eating (*haram*). Muslims are not allowed to eat the flesh of any animals that have died naturally or have not been specifically killed for food. They are also not allowed to consume blood, pork or any of its by-products (this may include some breads and yogurts), the flesh of animals slaughtered as sacrifices to pagan deities or not slaughtered in the *halal* fashion, any alcohol or fermented liquors.

Most Arabs understand that westerners live by a very different code of ethics (of which they are very critical) and that we could therefore eat foods that are not permitted to them and drink alcohol. It is, however, a mark of disrespect to eat or drink foods or beverages forbidden to them in their presence. Islam does lay down a series of rules to guide the behaviour of non-Muslims in Islamic countries. The general principle is that, if only westerners are present, they may do as they please, though only a fool would produce alcohol in, say, Saudi Arabia. The British Department of Trade and Industry says that 'purely British events in Arabia are conducted according to British rules,' but adds 'where Muslims are present it is polite to show regard for their sensitivities.'

Business practice and business etiquette
Just as it is wrong not to differentiate between the countries of the Arab world*, so it is wrong to assume that all adherents to the Islamic faith have the same outlook on religious or temporal affairs. The Saudi-Arabians view Islamic fundamentalists with suspicion. The Islamic fundamentalists, in turn, see those Arab states that are prepared to encourage peaceful relations with the west as traitors. Anyone from the west visiting an Arab country should first seek some understanding of the political and religious climate of opinion in that country. In general, the more strictly the Islamic code is applied in any country, the more carefully the western business visitor should prepare for his or (bravely) her trip, and the more circum-spectly the western visitor should exhibit respect for the

---

* There are over twenty different countries in what westerners refer to as the Arab world. As well as those already mentioned in this chapter, there are eight republics (Algeria, Djibouti – formerly French Somali-land, The Socialist People's Libyan Arab Jamahiriya, Mauritania, The Social Democratic Republic – formerly Somalia, Sudan, Tunisia and Yemen), three states (Bahrain, Kuwait and Qatar), the Kingdom of Morocco, the Sultanate of Oman, and the United Arab Emirates.

traditions and laws of the country.

For all the anxiety we may have about how we should behave in an Arab country, it's important to remember that the Arabs are a courteous people, famed for their hospitality. They will forgive much, especially many technical breaches of etiquette if there was no intention to show disrespect and if our general bearing and decorum are dignified and respectful.

Behaviour

The Arabs are a warm, friendly people. Arab men show friendship by touch a great deal more than men tend to in the west, but to touch a woman is an extreme breach of etiquette. It is customary to shake hands on meeting and leaving. The handshake in Arabia is more than a casual ritual. The hand may be held for some time, another sign of friendship. If the handshake we receive when we leave an Arab country is longer than the one we received on arrival, this is a sign that we have made a good impression. Such subtleties are part of the Arab way of life, and they resent people who lack subtlety. It is best never to force the notion of friendship on to an Arab, or to pretend that one exists where it clearly does not, or to assume that jocularity will carry the day and win hearts. The Arab way of life is much slower than that of the west.

There are certain golden rules of behaviour in Arab countries, the three most important of which are:

1. Never to cross legs (or even ankles) when in the presence of a ruler or someone in high authority. This is about as rude in Arab society as picking one's nose in public would be to us.
2. Never to allow the soles of our feet to point at anyone. This may require supple joints, but it's important to observe it. Traditionally, to present the soles of the feet has been a sign of contempt, and, even though there are signs that younger Arabs no longer regard it as such, it is best not to do so.

251

3. Never to use the left hand when accepting food or drink, or when actually eating or drinking. Traditional meals are eaten sitting on the floor. Cutlery is supplied, which may tempt us to use the left hand. Some find it helpful to sit on that hand, so that we can't use it. A spoon in the right hand is probably the easiest way to eat. The problem becomes considerably harder when eating a meal at a table, western style. We are then far more likely to forget. The rule may be relaxed, however, in some of the more progressive countries where it is permissible to use both hands when we are eating something where one hand simply isn't enough e.g. when peeling fruit.

All very difficult, especially since the Arabs are suspicious of someone who sits rigidly in one position with feet firmly anchored on the floor, every button done up, and sweating with formality. They prefer someone who appears relaxed and easy-going.

There are two other grave mistakes that we must avoid. One is to photograph military installations, airports, police barracks, prisons, government offices, embassies, power stations, mosques or Muslim women. The other is to discuss such Middle Eastern problems as the dispute between Israel and the Palestinians. No matter how sympathetic we may be towards the Israeli cause, we should never indicate any admiration for that country. Similarly, in Saudi Arabia it is a mistake to refer to the 'Persian Gulf'. Diplomatically speaking, the British Government would probably like us to refer to it simply as 'the Gulf', but an Arab will take it as a mark of respect if we refer to it as the 'Arabian Gulf'.

Business practices
The Arabs are not a punctual people. This doesn't mean that we should show ourselves to be life's loiterers, but we should expect delays to the start of any meetings. It is impolite to show any anger or frustration at such delays, however. To the

Arab there is plenty of time, and we must try to identify with that.

Once it gets under way, business is conducted at a slow pace. Again, there must be no display of temper at this. It's also a dreadful mistake to believe that things can be made to move more quickly by indulging in a little bribery. Westerners do not understand the Arab way of conducting business if we believe that bribery brings results. The only result it might bring is several months or years in gaol.

It is essential to have plenty of business cards, printed in English and Arabic (Persian, if we are going to Iran).

Meetings tend to be slow, relaxed and friendly. They are usually preceded by the serving of coffee. This may be anything from grey to yellow in colour, flavoured with spices. Small cups without handles are passed to each person present, and it is bad manners to decline to accept it. The coffee will be sweet. The correct procedure is to drink two of these tiny cups. In Saudi Arabia, to take only one is an insult, and to take three or more is greedy. When we wish for our second coffee, all we have to do is hold out the cup and it will be refilled. When we have had enough, we simply cover the cup with our hand and move it in a circular motion. A servant should then come to take the cup away.

If we are a newcomer to the company assembled for the meeting, then we shall be shown where to sit, and this will probably be next to the most important person present. This is both as a mark of respect and to put us at our ease. It is quite possible, however, that, as soon as another newcomer enters the room, we shall be moved so that he may sit next to the most important person present. All this may take a little time – we have to be patient.

Patience is essential in negotiations with Arabs. Any signs of emotional strain or impatience, any display of anger, any attempts to browbeat or to sell aggressively will be seen as marks of disrespect and signs of weakness. It's important also not to be thrown by what is normal behaviour at a business meeting. The Arabs often appear not to be paying attention during negotiations, their minds wandering, their gaze straying. This appearance is very deceptive. The Arabs are extremely able listeners, with a better recall of what was said than most westerners.

One oddity about business meetings in Arab countries is that the Arabs often invite people who have nothing to do with the negotiations taking place. This is simply so that these people may observe what is happening. It is rude to question why these people are present.

It is not necessary to be fluent in Arabic for business purposes. Most Arabs speak English well, partly a legacy of the British occupation. As in most countries, however, a knowledge of a few words of greeting helps and will be appreciated by our hosts.

Arab hospitality

As with business meetings, Arab hospitality is a slow, unhurried affair. It begins with an exchange of courtesies. It is correct to ask after the host's health and perhaps generally inquire after his family. It is not, however, polite to ask about his wife. We shouldn't interpret a silence as an embarrassed sign that nobody has anything to say. Pauses are frequent in Arab conversation, and may be a sign that much importance is being attached to the meeting or the conversation itself.

An Arab banquet is a sumptuous affair, with far more food served than the assembled company could possibly eat. Arabs who preserve the old traditional ways may not eat with their guests, but most Arabs will now join their guests at the table, or on the floor if it is a formal meal. Arab meals are often conducted in almost total silence, a sign that people are showing their appreciation for the food that has been set before them. This is perhaps just as well, for they are often much shorter in duration than an equivalent meal in the west – thirty or forty minutes is often thought long enough. Although there is always a great deal to eat, we should avoid any display of gluttony. A good appetite may be a healthy thing, but it is there to be controlled.

The banquet or meal may start with guests and hosts sitting together in a reception room (the *Marlis*). Here coffee and tea may be served, and a container of lighted incense is held towards the guests. The correct response in this circumstance is to waft the smoke from the container towards oneself with the right hand. After this has been done, rosewater is poured on the hands. It may sound simple enough, but such ceremonies may take over two hours, by which time a guest will have a healthy appetite for the meal itself.

An Arab host may well precede the meal by saying *Bismillah ar-Rahman ar-Rahim* (In the name of God, the Merciful, the Compassionate). If the meal is being eaten at the host's house, then guests may be invited to sit cross-legged on the floor. Once the meal begins, the host may not eat much himself, preferring to see that his guests are happy, and to offer them the choicest titbits that he can find from the food set before them. The food is eaten with the right hand only. No Muslim women will be present at the meal, and it is rare (though not unknown) for non-Muslim western women to be invited.

At the end of the meal, the host says 'Thanks be to God', and takes his guests to the door of his house, where he bids them farewell. It is polite, as guests, to show when we are ready to go. The traditional hospitality of the Arab would never permit him to show in any way that he considered it was time we left.

Women in the Arab world

At all the above, Arab women will not be present. Arab women entertain other women separately, usually in a more relaxed atmosphere, spending more time over a meal or in conversation. Western women (or non-Arab women) may attend banquets, receptions and other functions in theory. There is nothing in Arab law that forbids this, but the practicality of the situation does pose problems for Arabs, who find it difficult to know how to behave towards non-Arab women.

To get over this difficulty, in some Arab countries the term 'honorary male' has been invented. This means that non-Arab women will be treated in the same way as non-Arab men, with courtesy and hospitality. But there are still problems – Arab hosts are often unsure as to where women guests should sit at a formal dinner. The usual solution to the problem is to hold discussions beforehand on this point of etiquette. A common arrangement is to place all the host's party to the left of the host and all the host's guests to the right of the host. This way the non-Arab men and women will sit together, and any awkwardness the Arabs may feel about how to address and converse with women will be avoided.

In general, although there has been a considerable move towards what we should regard as the emancipation of women in many parts of the Arab world, there are still those countries where women lead traditional lives. In Saudi Arabia, for example, women still live in separate quarters from the men and do not receive male visitors. They are not allowed to drive cars. They must never appear in public unless they are wearing veils and full-length black robes. It is best for non-Arab men to be extremely circumspect in manner towards all Arab women. One way to avoid any breach of etiquette is to conduct all conversation with Arab women through an Arab male escort.

Gifts

It is essential to understand that in Arab society the presentation of a gift, no matter how innocently made, can present serious problems. This stems from the formal code of hospitality. By giving someone a present, we gain an advantage over them. We show that we know the rules of hospitality and place the recipient in a difficult position. Should he give an equally impressive present in return, and therefore appear to be trying to take away our advantage? Or should he give nothing, and therefore appear not to know the rules of hospitality himself? The swapping of presents complicates matters further, especially if it appears that each party is trying to appear more generous than the other.

Although there are some signs that Arabs are moving towards a more western philosophy of giving presents, i.e. exchanging gifts in public, it is better to adopt the traditional Arab way, which is to send presents anonymously at the end of a visit or a period of business negotiations. If we receive such an anonymous gift, we should not show that we have guessed whence it came by writing a letter of thanks. The whole thing should be kept secret.

One of the worst mistakes that a visitor to an Arab country can make is to express fulsome admiration for one of his host's possessions. To an Arab this imposes a duty. He feels bound by the rules of hospitality to make a present of the object in question to its admirer. However much we may protest and try to back down, the Arab host may insist that we keep it.

Dress
Visiting men and women to an Arab country should dress soberly. Suits, shirts and ties are best for men, and women should wear long dresses with long sleeves. In more progressive Arab countries it is permissible for women to wear slightly shorter dresses (but still covering the knees) and sleeves (but still covering the elbows). Women should not wear trousers. It is considered offensive for men to wear shorts or short-sleeved shirts in public, even when off-duty. On no account should men or women wear Arab dress.

CHAPTER 23

Business etiquette in the United States

Is it your intention to overthrow the Government of the United States by force?
QUESTION ON VISA APPLICATION FORM, 1950s

Sole purpose of visit
ANSWER FILLED IN BY GILBERT HARDING

Introduction
The United States is one of the biggest countries in the world. It is as far from New York to Los Angeles as it is from London to New York. We all know this, but we sometimes forget the significance of it. It has a population nearly five times that of Britain and is geographically thirty-eight times the size. It is culturally diverse. It is a mixture of different races, religions, languages, traditions. It is a salutary experience to visit the Museum of Immigration on Ellis Island in New York Harbour, and to learn a little of the variety of ethnic groups that have flocked there of their own free will, or been taken there by force over the centuries – Russians, Poles, Germans, Scandinavians, Scots, Irish, Vietnamese, Chinese, Indians, Japanese, South Americans, Africans, Lithuanians and many, many more. Different people have different codes of behaviour, so 'good manners' in Arkansas are not necessarily the same as 'good manners' in Chicago or California. Most Americans are proud of their country and their community, but they may well exhibit this pride in different ways. Wherever we go in the United States, it pays to do a little homework, to try to find out a little of the background and

259

history of the people that inhabit this particular state or city, county or town, and to remember that the United States is not one business market but many different markets.

Drive and determination

Although they still have a fundamental courtesy, the Americans are very critical of what seems indifference in the business world. To them, lack of preparation is impolite, and seems to denote a lack of care. Dealing in the United States is rather like having a small part in a play or film – we need to make our mark quickly for we may be on stage for only a little while. This means we have to make sure we have adequate up-to-date information about what we are seeking to buy or sell or negotiate, and we must know as much as possible about the potential market. Americans don't go naked, or semi-naked, into the conference room and they don't expect others to. Fortunately, information is always readily available in the United States. The US federal government is the world's largest collector of information, and Americans are far happier to share this information than most Europeans. They believe in freedom of information in the business world to a greater extent than is the practice in Britain, but it's no good expecting them to be so free with information as to cut their own throats. One helpful tip, if we wish to have access to information about any American company, is to buy a share or two in that company. It may also help our subsequent dealings to say we are shareholders in the company.

In general, the Americans prefer expensive or luxury quality goods and service – they are seldom in the market for the adequate and never for the shoddy. This means that all aspects of marketing, presentation and service must be of the highest order.

Communicating

Americans are also experts at communication. They invented the telephone, after all, and they use it in a brisk and businesslike way. It's bad manners to make a phone call to an American without being well prepared in what we are going to say. Time is money, and wasting time is one of the greatest sins in the American business world. We need to have our questions and facts and figures ready. We need to have done our preparatory research. We have to know to whom we wish to speak. Once we get to that person, we need to transmit well-organised thoughts. Charming prattle wins no contracts.

Americans are well established in the field of electronic communication generally. Fax machines are taken for granted and are essential, as most Americans demand written confirmation of any agreement made verbally, whether face-to-face or over the telephone. We need, therefore, to be on our toes, as US dealers expect immediate and accurate responses to any questions they wish to raise or points they wish to make. To dither is to seem rude as well as inefficient. In the words of Christopher Robinson, director of Lloyd's brokers Leslie and Godwin: 'If you say you will do something, you do it, and if you cannot you say why in plenty of time: in other words constant communication and no surprises.'

Also, because they invented market research, the American market is the most researched in the world. They are experts at what they can do or sell – they expect others to be, too. They admire the hard sell, aggressive dealing, but they don't admire or accept rudeness. Americans like to be questioned intelligently. They like to be helpful and feel frustrated if we don't allow them that chance through our own bumbling inefficiency. They are the mothers and the fathers of public relations, and they're very good at it. They like their personal portraits or profiles in trade magazines and publicity brochures to be warmer, friendlier. A flat, bald account of schools and colleges attended, qualifications gained and positions held seems stand-offish to them. American business people like to be portrayed as parents, partners, members of the local community, amateur sportspeople, as well as executive vice-presidents.

The quality of the pitch

America is the land of first impressions, so they had better be good ones. In the US the quality of the product and everything to do with it is important. Photocopies should be sharp and crisp, not grey besmudged poor relations of the original document. Brochures and sales literature and back-up material should be professionally presented, whether it's video tapes, product samples, packaging, etc. And Americans don't always mean by 'sample', a minuscule giveaway – sometimes a sample in the US has to be the same size as a normal order in Britain.

Because there are so many rivals all bidding for the same order, American customers tend to select and buy from the individual rather than the company. This puts a premium on courtesy at all times. It is rare for an American to refuse to see a salesman, but he or she will welcome efficiency, a good pitch and a quick exit.

Language problems

It pays to remember George Bernard Shaw's famous remark that 'America and Britain are two countries divided by a common language.' Americans notice and appreciate when sales literature or business letters have been translated into their language, when 'colour' has become 'color', when a 'station' has become a 'depot', a 'lorry' a 'truck', a 'railway' a 'railroad', a 'motorway' a 'highway' (or, better, a 'state highway'), 'labour' has become 'labor', and a 'factory' a 'plant'. More to the point, it is bad practice not to translate technical details into American measurements. All technical specifications should be in American English, and all prices quoted should always be in dollars. Confusion may be created if we do not use American notation for dates on letters and documents. 5.10.94 may mean 5th October 1994 to us, but it means 10th May to them.

However swiftly we may become fed up with 'How are you today?' and 'Have a nice day!', the naggingly ubiquitous *salve et valete* of every shop, diner, bar, gas station and complete

262

stranger in the United States, the sentiments and concern for visitors to their country are often genuinely felt by Americans, and to ridicule them is to risk giving grave offence.

What seems big and important in Britain may seem very small and insignificant 3000, 6000 or even 7000 miles away. We have to look outside the confines of our own sceptred isle. If we wish to refer to, say, Oxford, do we mean Oxford, Alabama, Idaho, Indiana, Iowa, Kansas, Maine, Maryland, Massachusetts, Michigan, Mississippi, North Carolina, Nebraska, New York, Ohio, or Wisconsin? Or are we referring to Oxford, Nova Scotia? Or New Zealand? They all exist, and Americans may not necessarily assume that we mean *the* one, in England.

Stationery obstacles

If possible, we should try to make sure all our brochures, hand-outs, sales literature etc., is printed on American size stationery. Americans do not use the A4 size that is common in Britain. They prefer American quarto size (11 inches by 8 1/2 inches). It's important to use this size, as this is what fits their folders and files. Business cards are also often a different size in the United States (usually 3 1/2 inches by 2 inches). It is advisable to put first name as well as family name on such cards – Americans regard lack of first name as a mark of frigidity or pomposity or simply unfriendliness.

Bad times to do business

It is a mark of lack of respect not to be aware of business hours and business days in the United States. Many people start work early in the day, and work through until well into the evening. Their time away from the office is, therefore, very precious, and shouldn't be intruded upon lightly. It is also important to know the time differences between Britain and the various American time zones when making a telephone call. Nobody likes to be woken in the middle of the night to be given the latest quotations from Prestige Pumps.

There are four different time zones in the United States:

EASTERN ZONE: This covers the area inland from the Atlantic to the Great Lakes and the Appalachian Mountains. It's five hours behind Greenwich Mean Time, so 12 noon London time is 07.00 hours in New York. The time in this zone is referred to as Eastern Standard Time.

CENTRAL ZONE: This covers the central mass of the United States, from Chicago in the north to Texas in the south, from Illinois in the east to Kansas in the west. It's six hours behind Greenwich Mean Time, and the time in this zone is referred to as Central Standard Time.

MOUNTAIN ZONE: This covers the Rocky Mountains and the south western states. It's seven hours behind Greenwich Mean Time, and the time in this zone is referred to as Mountain Standard Time.

PACIFIC ZONE: This includes four states – Washington, Oregon, California and Nevada. It's eight hours behind Greenwich Mean Time, and the time in this zone is referred to as Pacific Standard Time.

Alaska and Hawaii have times of their own. Both states are ten hours behind Greenwich Mean Time. Daylight Saving Time approximates to that in Britain.

It also helps to be aware of the main public holidays in the United States, which are:

New Years Day	1 January
Martin Luther King Day	mid-January (varies from year to year)
Washington's Birthday	mid-February (strangely, this varies, too)
Independence Day	4 July
Labor Day	early September
Thanksgiving Day	late November
Christmas Day	25 December

264

Visitors to the United States should also try to make themselves aware of days that are sacred to certain sportsmen.
Don't expect to do a great deal of business in Kentucky the
day the deer-hunting season opens.

Regulation and legislation

It is bad practice and bad manners not to be aware of the,
admittedly, complex US legislation covering packaging and
labelling of goods in the United States, and not to keep up to
date with changes in rules and regulations. It suggests a woeful
lack of interest. Any manufacturer, for example, who submits
a product for approval in the United States – so that it may be
marketed – should have the most up-to-date information
regarding testing, registration, trade standards, what phraseol-
ogy or claims may or may not be used in advertising copy, etc.
The United States may seem a very cut-and-thrust market, but
in many ways, it's far more strictly regulated than the European market. Not to have this information may justifiably
offend officials, as well as clients or customers. Admittedly,
this is not an easy task, but regular and persistent enquiries
will enable most companies to keep abreast of the complex
and ever-changing trade laws of the United States.

Since Americans are reckoned to be the most litigious
people in the world, it helps to know something of the
American legal system. The Americans may have taken their
language from the British, but they took most of their
constitution and legal system from the French. Legal advisers
in the United States play a significant role in business. The
presence of a lawyer in negotiations (where one would not
normally appear in Britain) is not an unsubtle hint that our
American business partners don't trust us. It is standard
practice. And we shouldn't be surprised or offended at the
important role legal advisers play in negotiations. To the
Americans, lawyers are not there merely as legal technicians.
They are fully fledged members of the negotiating team, for
Americans know that close attention has to be paid to the
huge amount of legislation that covers business conduct in the

United States – much more so than in Britain. The corollary of this is that we in turn should be prepared to have our own legal advisers present at such meetings.

Patience is needed to comply with contract law and practice in the United States. Americans like their contracts to be meticulously detailed – every loophole closed, every eventuality covered. Once that has been done, as far as they are concerned, the right atmosphere has been created for a friendly working partnership. So we should expect a contract to contain at least the following:

1. Delivery price.
2. Method of delivery.
3. Terms covering late delivery.
4. Standard of goods to be supplied.
5. Conditions covering any failure to meet these standards.
6. What should happen in the event of labour problems.
7. What should happen if only part of the order is delivered.
8. How the law should be applied in the event of any of the above problems.
9. How the law should be applied in the event of any unforeseen problems.
10. Almost anything else.

It is better to come clean at the earliest possible moment if any of the terms of the contract cannot be fulfilled. If an American customer asks for a certain delivery date and this cannot be met, we should say so, preferably before the contract is signed. It may be that the customer is prepared to give extra time.

Culture and history
The United States has existed for a little over two hundred years, since British colonial rule came to an end after the War of Independence in the late 18th century. American

independence was recognised by the Treaty of Versailles in 1783. To us dear old Europeans this may seem almost the day before yesterday, but Americans are a traditional people, and they are proud of traditions that may go back little more than living memory. An 'old established' firm in their eyes may have been founded as recently as the 1960s. It doesn't do to mock such a perspective.

Despite the historical differences of opinion (we did go to war with the United States again in 1812, and many British industrialists and politicians backed the losing side in the War Between the States 1861–1865), Americans are used to business dealing with Britain. The United States has a huge concentration of foreign direct investment, 28% of which is British (the Japanese have the second biggest contribution, only 18%), but this happy state of affairs should not be taken for granted.

The United States is proud of its culture and its industry and very protective towards both, so news of the 630% increase in foreign direct investment in the 1980s came as something of a shock to many Americans. The 'Exon-Florio' component of the 1988 Trade Act provided the President of the United States with the authority to suspend or prohibit any acquisition, merger, or take-over of a US business by a foreigner on certain national security grounds. In other words, the Americans can be as protective as anyone towards their own industries. It doesn't do, however, to taunt them with charges of hypocrisy on the basis of their loud disapproval of France's recent highly protectionist attitude towards her own film industry.

Accusations of hypocrisy are not considered good manners in any country.

Local pride

It is very important in the United States to respect local pride and local achievements. The Americans have far more civic pride and community awareness than the British. They are nearer to the French in this respect. At state, county and town level, Americans are proud of their schools, churches, public buildings, highways, bridges, railroad stations, shopping malls, parks and playgrounds. They elect their own local officials – school board, sheriff, governor, district attorney. If we condemn or pour scorn on such people, we are indirectly mocking the system by which they were elected, and the people who elected them. We may think that the Americans have done much to poison and pollute a beautiful country (who are we to talk), but such sentiments are best left un- or very sensitively expressed.

It pays to remember that there are over 1600 local daily newspapers in the United States and only a couple of national ones, and that Americans are therefore unlikely to take a national view of internal affairs. Their opinions on the economy, trade, the environment, communications, etc. will be largely determined by the state or county in which they live. Only in their views of what should happen in the rest of the world are Texans, Californians and New Yorkers likely to unite.

Although the United States has a close identification of interest with Britain for much of the time, the two nations do not always think alike. The United States is warmer in its attitude towards some countries and colder towards others than Britain, maintaining strictly critical views of Cambodia, Cuba, Haiti, Iran, Iraq, Libya, North Korea, some of the former Soviet republics and Vietnam, among others. It should not be assumed that any and every American will share our approval or disapproval of ally and rival or enemy respectively.

Race, colour and creed
Such religious and racial integration or toleration as exists in Britain may be as much the result of the passage of time as of pressure groups and legislation. We've had hundreds of years in which to find ways of allowing Jews, Catholics, Protestants and others to live peacefully side by side. The Americans have fought hard over a much shorter period to bring together their

different religions, races and cultures. They take a very dim view of infringements of civil rights, conduct that so much as veers towards discrimination, or sexual harassment. Many people gave their lives in more ways than one in the struggle to bring justice, liberty and equality to all, not hundreds of years ago, but in the very, very recent past.

Americans are, therefore, jealous of the cornerstones of their constitution and of the ideals embodied in the Declaration of Independence way back in 1776. In Britain we have no similar written embodiment of political ideals, but probably there are proportionately as many Americans who can quote from the Declaration of Independence or the Gettysberg Address that followed it in 1863 as there are British people who know the words of *Rule Britannia*. Abraham Lincoln's words still mean a great deal to an enormous number of Americans today, and it is impolite to remind them that he also said 'You can fool all the people some of the time, and some of the people all the time, but you cannot fool all the people all the time.'

Through American eyes
Because of the huge size of the United States, there is sometimes a problem for visitors in making their visit to any one town, business or individual seem little more than just another fleeting stop-off among many on a busy schedule. It is all too easy to give the impression that calling on Walter's Processed Foods is incidental to some other, more important purpose. The way to avoid this is to recognise what Americans regard as important, what they value in business.

Americans appreciate modesty, but this can be a two-edged weapon, and faint heart never won fair contract. They don't like cringing humility. They like someone who is gently but firmly persuasive about the quality of what he or she has to offer.

They like efficiency. They invented fast food, freeways, the modern factory assembly system, the moving staircase and almost every modern marketing technique. They

269

admire perseverance – they invented the non-stop dance competition and the twenty-six-part television series. They approve of adaptability – 'It's your burger – you can have it any way you want'. They appreciate a sense of humour – sharing a two-minute joke with a stranger in the United States gets us as close as a two-year acquaintance does in Britain. And, above all, they like intelligence. Americans are quick-witted, imaginative and verbally adept – they use language like ingredients in cooking, constantly creating new phrases, expressions, images.

Index

271